'Scott is the rarest of one-two punches, having a wonderful understanding of both the creative and business sides of the publishing industry. If I could give you one bit of advice, it'd be to shut up and listen to everything he has to say. If I could give you two bits of advice, it'd be that, plus: people getting punched in the groin is never not funny.'
Caimh McDonnell, bestselling author of *The Dublin Trilogy*

'Scott has championed me from the very start of my self-published writing career. In 2011 he quoted that I was as good if not better than any traditionally published romcom author. As I sit at No 1 in the Kindle bestselling chart, I guess he knows what he's talking about.'
Nicola May, No 1 bestselling author of *The Corner Shop in Cockleberry Bay*

'Few people in the publishing world can claim to have such wide and varied knowledge and experience of so many aspects of the industry. As a publisher, bookseller, author and speaker (not necessarily in that order), Scott not only has the breadth and depth of experience to impart but he does so forthrightly and with great humour. I wouldn't trust anyone else to give me advice, he really knows his stuff!'
Valerie Brandes, founder, Jacaranda Books

'Scott has unrivalled experience as a book buyer, editor and publisher; he's seen and done it all from across the business. If you want to know about any aspect of the book world, what he says really does matter and will make a huge difference.'
Michael Bhaskar, co-founder and publishing director, Canelo

'Scott is a rare beast who combines pragmatic commerciality with creative flair and sensitivity, all wrapped in a no-BS, tell-it-how-it-is persona. His short cuts on how to win are invaluable guides not only on how to get published but also how to sell books. Unfortunately if he thinks your magnum opus is crap he will happily tell you so.'
David Roche, former Chief Executive, Borders UK & Ireland

'Not only is Scott Pack the best editor I've worked with, but as a publisher, he's erudite, passionate and creative – must-have qualities every successful publisher should combine.'
Ray Robinson, author of *The Mating Habits of Stags*

'From being the key national bookseller at Waterstones to becoming a publisher and champion of digital publishing, the inveterate enthusiast Scott Pack has long been a highly regarded and influential figure in the book trade.'
Charley Viney, The Viney Shaw Agency

'Scott is truly wise about all aspects of the publishing process and industry. He's also a tiny bit irreverent, which means he will always tell it how it is.'
Abi Silver, author of the Burton & Lamb crime series

'A book-shaped boot camp for emerging writers. Essential reading for creative writing students everywhere.'
Judith Heneghan, director, Winchester Writers' Festival

'Part instruction manual, part sat nav, part friendly arm round the shoulder: this is the book every aspiring writer needs to own.'
John Mitchinson, co-founder & Chief Publishing Officer, Unbound

'Scott is known in the publishing industry for his straight-talking approach – he can be relied upon for sensible and honest advice.'
Angus Phillips, director, Oxford International Centre for Publishing

'Scott is a damn fine editor.'
Paul Dodgson, author of *On the Road Not Taken*

'I had the pleasure of working with Scott at HarperCollins and I learned a huge amount from him. As well as possessing a deep understanding of the business of publishing books, he is also forward-thinking and knows exactly how latest innovations can impact his work effectively. Scott brings a hell of a lot to the party.'
Sam Missingham, founder, Lounge Marketing

'Scott knows the publishing industry inside-out and whenever I work with him, I know my authors are in good hands.'
Charlotte Seymour, literary agent

Tips
from a
Publisher

A GUIDE TO
WRITING, EDITING, SUBMISSIONS AND MORE

S C O T T
P A C K >

Published by Eye Books
29A Barrow Street
Much Wenlock
Shropshire
TF13 6EN

www.eye-books.com

First edition 2020
Copyright © Scott Pack 2020

Cover design by Ifan Bates
Copyedit and typesetting by Clio Mitchell
Proofreading by Alan Smithee

A version of 'The Mathematics of Publishing' chapter has previously appeared in *The Writers' and Artists' Yearbook*. A version of the 'How to Perfect Your Submission' chapter has previously been published as a separate ebook. Versions of many of the other chapters have appeared on screwed-up bits of paper in the bin next to Scott's desk.

British Library Cataloguing in Publication Data

A catalogue record for this book is available from the British Library

Printed by CPI Group (UK) Ltd, Croydon CR0 4YY

ISBN 9781785631443

This book is dedicated to every author
who ever wrote a wonderful book that went unnoticed,
or didn't find a publisher, or did get published
but didn't sell nearly as well as it should have done,
or went out of print, or was otherwise neglected.

And here's to those books being rediscovered some day.

Contents

Foreword

An Introduction to the Publishing World

Writing Your Book

Revising Your Book

Submitting and Publishing Your Book

Extras

Foreword

I have spent twenty years working in the book world – first as head of buying for the Waterstones book chain, then as a publisher, spending eight years at HarperCollins, and latterly as a freelance editor – and I think it is fair to say that they have been twenty of the most eventful years in the history of the industry.

We have seen the rise of Amazon and its resultant global domination as well as the – clearly linked – demise of many traditional book retailers, both big and small. There has been the development of ebooks as a popular reading format and the revolution in self-publishing that has come about as a result. Some of the biggest publishers in the world have merged or bought each other to become even bigger, and independent publishers have become more creative and imaginative to compete with them. Social media has changed the way readers share their love, or loathing, of books while traditional print media just about limps on, albeit with a vastly reduced level of influence, especially when it comes to book reviews.

Pretty much everything has changed, perhaps not quite beyond recognition but enough to give everyone in the world of publishing and bookselling a bloody good shake-up. However, one thing has remained constant, one thing that I don't believe will ever really change, and that is the simple fact that the world is full of unpublished writers who want to be published. And despite the many and increased options available to them, the majority want to be published in the traditional fashion, with an agent representing them and a publisher producing their books and selling them in bookshops.

But here's something that has always struck me as strange: the publishing world tends to keep authors at arm's length as much as possible. Unpublished authors have to navigate, alone, the fraught world of the submissions process – often receiving nothing but standard, anonymous rejections for their trouble – before they can even get a whiff of publication. And once they do get a publishing deal, they are rarely, if ever, allowed anywhere near the many meetings and discussions – editorial, marketing, publicity, sales – that will decide their fate. Consequently, much of the industry is shrouded in mystery. It is inaccessible and hard to break into. It comes across as elitist and insular. Myths start to develop. Writers get obsessed with being part of the next trend. Unpublished authors, often desperate to get a deal, make myriad mistakes because they just don't know how the whole thing works.

But it doesn't have to be this way.

This book is designed to break down those barriers, smash those myths and open up the closed world of the book industry to writers at any stage in their careers, although I assume it will appeal most to aspiring authors, unpublished writers and those just venturing out on a literary career.

The book is split into five main sections, with lots of subsections in between, and can be read from start to finish – it will make chronological sense that way – or you can dip in and out depending on your areas of interest.

The first section, 'An Introduction to the Publishing World', does precisely what the title suggests. It explains how the book world works, looks at the processes that go into producing a printed book, the numbers that drive the industry – sales figures, costs, royalties etc. – and explains the various publishing models that are available to authors. It is my belief that the more a writer knows about what goes on behind the scenes in publishing, the easier it will be for them to break into it.

The second section, 'Writing Your Book', delves into the actual writing of a book and is packed full of the advice I give authors almost every day in my role as an editor. It is not intended as a comprehensive writing guide – this book covers too many areas to focus in detail on that – but I do look at elements of writing fiction, such as characterisation, dialogue, plot and world-building, as well as offering strategies for getting a book, whether fiction or non-fiction, written and completed.

This is followed by 'Revising Your Book', a look at the process of rewriting, re-drafting and editing your work, how to knock it into shape ready for submission and publication.

'Submission & Publication' is, conveniently enough, the next section. It explores what happens once your book is written, mainly focusing on the submissions process – how best to present your work to agents and publishers to give it the greatest chance of being picked up – but also delving into the world of self-publishing and some of the practicalities of life as an author.

We end up with a section I have called 'Extras' that contains all the stuff that didn't quite fit in anywhere else, including templates, checklists, and resources covering all aspects of writing.

And sprinkled throughout the book are little asides, called 'A Few Words About...', which focus in on key aspects of writing and publishing that deserve a bit more attention or discussion.

I want this book to help you, the writer, become better equipped to explore, navigate and survive within the book world. I can't be sure that your book is a work of genius, but I can ensure that it, and you, have the best possible chance of success. After all, if you want to know how publishing works, you might as well ask a publisher.

An Introduction to the Publishing World

This opening section of the book is intended as a guided tour, albeit a whistle-stop one, of the world of publishing. I firmly believe that authors should understand how the industry works before they dive headfirst into it, or even just dip their toe in gingerly. Much of what I am about to tell you is rarely shared with authors, in fact some of it is actively hidden from them, but I want you to be as well prepared as possible for what lies ahead.

I will walk you through the life-cycle of a book from the point at which you type THE END to the day that your magnum opus appears on bookshop shelves, I shall explain the many different business models that operate within publishing, and I will share the numbers that drive the finances of our industry. It may not all make for comfortable reading, but it is essential information if you are going to be able to navigate the world of publishing.

1

The Life-cycle
of a Book

Perhaps the best way to start our guided tour of the world
of publishing is by examining the life-cycle of a book. What
is the process that takes the words you have typed on your
computer and turns them into a printed book, a book that
will sit along other real, actual books on the shelves of a
bookshop? What are the individual stages, how do they
work, and how does the author fit in to the whole thing?

Manuscript

Every book begins its life as an idea inside a writer's head but
at some point, often after months or years of prevarication,
or of life getting in the way, it makes its way onto the page.

And no matter how you write your first draft – quill and ink, biro on paper, thumbs on a smartphone or tapping fingers on a computer keyboard – you will at some point end up with a computer file containing your manuscript.

Elsewhere in this book I explore the whole submissions process in great detail but, for now, let's assume that you have already digested that splendid chapter, have perfected your submission, and your manuscript is out with a number of agents. And what is more, for the purposes of this illustration we are going to assume that they love it and want to sign you up.

Congratulations. Exciting, and occasionally confusing, times lie ahead.

The agent and the deal

Usually the first person to get to grips with a writer's manuscript, other than the writer themselves, is an agent. Agents receive hundreds, if not thousands, of manuscripts every week and trawl through them to find the ones that appeal to them, that they think show great talent and potential and that they can sell to publishers and make money from. I look at how agents work and what they do in more detail in the next chapter of this book but for now the important thing to know is that an agent is someone who has contacts throughout the publishing world and will know which publishers and editors are most likely to want to publish your book. Their job is to get your manuscript in front of those people and persuade them to sign it up, and they are better placed to do this than most authors.

But before they do, they are highly likely to want to edit your manuscript, to help you knock it into shape. These days an agent is often an author's first professional editor and you can expect some weeks, perhaps even months, of tweaks and new drafts before they feel the book is ready to send out. Once it is ready, they will begin their quest to find you a publisher.

Your manuscript will now be pinging its way into the email inboxes of a select band of editors at publishing houses, together with an encouraging email from your agent. The tone and content of the email will depend on the realistic expectations your agent has for the book. If they feel it is a guaranteed blockbuster and deserves a whopping advance then they will only have sent it out to a few high-flying editors with big chequebooks, perhaps with a strict deadline for offers. Of course, for most authors this is not the case and the agent will have sent the manuscript to a handful of editors they think, based on their tastes and track records, will a) like the book, and b) be prepared to publish it. Once sent, they will sit back and wait for a response.

And wait. And wait. Just like agents, editors receive an overwhelming amount of submissions and they can only read so much in any given day. As a result, agents may have to wait a few weeks, sometimes even a couple of months, for a response and that response may not be positive – but it is far too early in the book to have any negative thoughts so let's assume your agent has found an eager publisher. You have moved one step closer to seeing your book in your local bookshop. Crack open the fizzy wine or, at the very least, treat yourself to a cup of tea and a slice of cake.

Editing

Despite what the job title suggests, editors at publishing houses don't do anywhere near as much editing as you'd think. At least, many of them don't. This isn't meant as a slight on them in any way, it is just a realistic reflection of how the business works these days. An editor – by which I mean the person who works for a publisher acquiring books and nursing them through to print – is more of a project manager than someone with a big red pen painstakingly marking up every little problem in your manuscript. They will perform some sort of edit, almost certainly, but this is likely to be a broader, structural edit, or a detailed read with notes, perhaps fine-tuning some of the things you will have already worked on with your agent. They want to help you make the book as good as it can be but it is unlikely they will have acquired the book if they felt it needed loads of work to get it there.

However detailed or involved the editor's work may be, and however many rewrites, new drafts or little fiddles this involves, at some point they will feel the manuscript is ready for the next stage, which is, I am sure you'll be delighted to discover, another edit.

A copyedit comes next. This is where someone, often a

freelancer employed by the publisher purely to copyedit manuscripts as and when needed, goes through the book and flags up anything that is just plain wrong. Copyeditors are usually wonderful pedants who enjoy fixing the incorrect use of grammar, pointing out where a semicolon would be better than a comma, or an en-dash is needed to replace a hyphen, and so on. They also tend to pick up on plot and character inconsistencies – she was wearing a green coat earlier in the chapter and now it is red, for example. And they will have no fear about getting stuck into an individual sentence if they feel that a bit of rejigging or hitting the delete button will improve the clarity of the text, or help with the reading flow. They may also comment on broader issues, hangovers from the structural edits that have already taken place, if they feel strongly about something, but essentially the copyedit is a wash and brush-up of the text so that it is fit for purpose and ready to be turned into a book. It is important to stress that the author gets to see all of these proposed changes and can make a case for not implementing some of them if there is a good reason not to.

Up till now, edits have been relatively easy, and cheap, to make – just a case of farting around with a Word document, really – but from this point on, and as your book gets closer to becoming a print edition, making changes is more difficult and costs more money to do. Which is why it is so important to have a good structural edit, followed by a thorough copyedit, to eradicate the need for too many alterations later on.

The length of time these two edits can take will differ from book to book, from editor to editor, and from author to author but, allowing for some back and forth and consultation, you can expect a structural edit to take two to three months, and a copyedit can usually be turned around in under a month.

Typesetting

Now that the manuscript is as close to perfect as can be, it needs to be turned into a book.

Although most word-processing software offers you lots of fancy fonts, and you can make all manner of layout changes, you will probably have noticed that the text in a book looks a bit different to the text on the last Word document you worked on. This is because a professional typesetter has, well, typeset it.

In olden times, this would actually involve a printer individually setting blocks of type on a printing press, ready to print the pages of the book. Hence the name: typesetting. These days, of course, it is all done on a computer, often with a piece of software called InDesign, but still with human input. The human will choose a font[1], apply that across the whole manuscript and then muck about with it for a while to make sure it looks good.

When I say 'muck about with it for a while', what I actually mean is that they will check each line on each page to ensure

---

1   There are many fonts used by publishers and some publishers will consult the author in the choice of font. The book you are reading now has been set using Garamond for most of the text.

the layout flows correctly. They are looking out for words that carry over from one line to another and have therefore been hyphenated (to avoid them if possible or, at least, make sure there aren't too many of them), for paragraphs where the first line starts at the very bottom of a page or where the last line carries over to a new page (known as 'widows' and 'orphans') as these are seen as untidy. Such issues can rarely be eradicated completely but a typesetter will attempt to keep them to a minimum. They will also be aiming to keep to a certain page count – every additional page costing the publisher more money – and implementing any special design features the author or editor may have requested, such as the light-grey typewriters you see in the background of the opening page of each section in this book.

They achieve all this by subtle manipulation of the text, such as reducing the space between words, until everything looks hunky dory. And then we are nearly finished, but we'll want to double-check everything first.

The typesetting process doesn't usually take very long, and a publisher will typically receive a typeset manuscript within a week or so of sending it to the typesetter.

Proofreading

Although the typesetter has presumably done a damn fine job with your book, they won't actually have read it. They are only interested in the layout of the words, not the story the words convey. It is also possible that while manipulating the text they may have introduced a few accidental typos or errors. So it is important that the whole thing gets one more read before any copies are printed.

The typesetter will have provided the publisher with a PDF of the manuscript, often known as 'page proofs', which is then passed on to a proofreader. In another example of a literal job title, a proofreader reads the proofs to look for errors. They study each word on each page to ensure it is spelt correctly, also looking out for errors in punctuation or layout, checking for anything that isn't quite right.

Some proofreaders still print the manuscript onto paper and mark it up by hand, using a set of long-established proofing marks that look like a cross between Pitman's shorthand and Egyptian hieroglyphs, but these days most do it all electronically, with the publisher receiving a tracked array of suggested corrections marked directly onto the document file.

It is fairly common practice for the author to also receive a copy of the typeset manuscript at some point, either at the same time as the proofreader or once the proofread has been completed. This will be the final chance for you to make any changes, although any *major* text changes at this stage are actively discouraged as they could affect the layout and pagination.

Although the time it takes for the proofread will depend on the length of the book, it is rarely more than a week or two at the most.

Once the publisher has confirmed all the corrections then the typesetter ensures they are all implemented and your book is more or less ready to go.

Cover

So far, everything we have explored in the life-cycle of a book has been a series of consecutive stages – agent finds editor, editor edits book, copyeditor fixes the text, the text is typeset, proofreader corrects any typos – but some parts of the process take place while others are happening, and creation of the book's cover is one of them.

An editor will usually brief a designer on the sort of cover they want fairly soon after the contract is signed. Having a rough idea of how the finished book will look is hugely helpful when championing the book in-house to the sales and marketing teams and externally to booksellers and media.

It is also a good idea to get cracking on the cover pretty early because everyone and their dog will have an opinion on it and it can take weeks, sometimes months, of fiddling to get it right. And even then not everyone will like it.

The process of designing a cover usually starts with a written brief from the editor. This will outline to the designer, who may never actually read the book, how the editor wants the finished cover to look. Sometimes this will be very precise – there is an agreed photograph to use, a preferred font for the text, a particular colour template to follow – and at other times it may offer the designer room for interpretation. The sort of things a cover brief would ideally include are: a brief summary of the story, a list of key features such as location, era, character descriptions, the type of reader you are aiming to sell the book to and examples of similar covers in the same genre. It may also feature a mood board, a series of images that capture the mood and feel you are looking for and could help prompt the designer in their search for inspiration.

The designer will then go away, weave their magic, and come back with some rough ideas for a front cover. This might be just one design, if they are confident they have nailed the brief, or it could be a few different treatments. Either way, the options will be considered by the editor, as well as the sales and marketing teams, and feedback given to the designer – a list of suggested tweaks or changes. With most publishers it would be highly unlikely for the author to get to see any of the options at this stage.

Rather a lot of back and forth now tends to ensue, often depending on a) how good the brief was in the first place, and b) how annoying the editor's sales and marketing colleagues are being[2], but, eventually, a consensus will be reached. It is often only at this point that the author gets to see the cover. Sometimes (trade secret alert!), if the editor wants to be a bit sneaky, they will show the author the 'final' cover alongside a couple of the early rejected drafts. That way the preferred cover stands out as much better than the others and the theory is that the author will gravitate towards it, but it can be a risky strategy if the author falls head over heels in love with one of the others. More often, the author is shown the agreed cover along with a very excited pep talk from the editor explaining that everyone in-house loves it and why

---

2   Can you tell I used to be an editor sitting through endless cover meetings at a big publishing house? Not that I am bitter or remotely scarred by the experience. Not at all.

the sales team believes it will be a hit with retailers, etc. This is more of a friendly 'dislike this at your peril' strategy.

If the patron saint of editors is in a good mood that day, the author will be pleased with the proposed cover and may have a few minor suggestions (which won't always include 'Can my name be bigger?' but often does) that are easy enough to accommodate. Things become more problematic when the author hates the idea or has pages of requested amendments. However, most publishing contracts have a specific clause when it comes to covers, stating that the publisher has final say. It is not unheard of for a book to hit bookshops with a cover the author hates, but usually the cover is something everyone involved has broad agreement over.

Once the thumbs up has been obtained, the designer goes away and turns the agreed front cover into a full cover, with spine, back cover complete with blurb, logos, barcode, price and so on.

Having read through this lengthy explanation it won't surprise you to learn that the cover design process can take several months to complete, and that is why it tends to run alongside many of the other early stages of production. The crucial thing is that a final cover is in place by the time the sales team starts to sell the book to retailers.

Sales

It is all very well to produce a wonderful book and plonk a beautiful cover on the front but you also have to sell the bloody thing. Most medium- to large-sized publishers have a dedicated in-house sales team who are in regular contact with the big retailers and wholesalers, keeping them updated on forthcoming titles, as well as the performance of new and existing ones, and doing their best to get decent orders. Smaller publishers may only have one sales person, or may use an external sales agency to do a similar job. I look in more detail at the retail model later in the book so if you are a sales geek there will be fun to be had shortly.

The important thing to understand for now is that retailers like to know what books are coming many months ahead. In the UK this is typically three to six months before a book is published. In the US it can be as much as nine to twelve months. This is why publishers do their best to have a finished cover, and a close-to-final text, way ahead of publication. It is also one of the reasons that publishing and the book world can often seem a bit slow and old-fashioned. It is certainly why Amazon has been able to revolutionise self-publishing with its ability to help authors bring books to market within a few hours, rather than the several months it takes if you are tied to the traditional model: if the lead times bookshops insist upon are slowing things down, just remove bookshops from the equation.

But, for now, if you want to be published traditionally,

you need to follow the traditional rules, and that means the sales team, or sales person, will have all the details of your book months ahead of publication and will present them to retailers in the hope of an order. Do bear in mind, though, that yours will usually be just one of several books being sold in, and the priority your book is given will be largely out of your hands. If a publisher has paid a massive advance for your book then they need to sell bucket-loads to make back their investment, so you can be sure that they'll make it a top priority when selling to retailers, pushing for a decent order. If, however, your book was acquired for little or no advance, then they won't be under the same sort of budgetary pressures, and you are reliant on a vociferous editor championing your book in-house to ensure it is given a fair crack.

Things are somewhat different with small and independent publishers, where your book may be the only one they are publishing that month. Wonderful stuff, you get 100% of their attention. The downside is that that one book from a solitary indie publisher is vying against all the other books the retailer has been presented from all the other publishers. So it is understandably hard to stand out from the crowd.

The sales team will be involved to some extent with many of the previous phases of the book, having a say in acquisition and cover design and blurb, but they really come into their own in that crucial retail window when bookshops are considering future titles. They will do their best to sell as many copies of your book as possible. And all of the above process takes place without any direct input from the author.

In fact, the majority of published authors probably still don't really know how the sales side of things works. You are now ahead of them on that score.

Marketing and publicity

Although marketing and publicity are two separate and distinct functions, most publishers keep them under one roof as parts of the same department. For small publishers both areas may be handled by just the one person.

There are many broad, as well as subtle, differences between the two, but to keep things simple here's a rather basic explanation.

Marketing is promotional activity that costs money and is usually spent to tell the general public that a book is available to buy. Press advertising, posters at train stations or on the sides of buses, billboards – that sort of thing. It rarely involves the author at all.

Publicity is activity that costs more time than money and not only tells the public that a book is available to buy, but hopefully prompts some reaction to it and discussion about it. It can often involve the author directly. Press and radio interviews, appearances on TV show sofas (which obviously would need the author's involvement), as well as newspaper reviews, blog reviews and the like, which don't always need anything from the author.

Marketing costs money and, as such, tends to be reserved for established authors, big-name brands, and debuts for which the publisher has spent way too much on the advance. With all due respect to my lovely readers, you are not currently one of those authors so we can gloss over this and move on.

Publicity is a different matter, and nearly every book published will be subject to some level of publicity. Ideally, there will be a bespoke plan which identifies which television and radio shows might want to interview the author, which newspapers will review the book, which bloggers, Instagrammers, YouTubers and Tweeters might love it and want to shout about it, and early copies[3] of the book will be sent to them, together with a publicity pack or press release, in the hope that they will feature it. A good publicity person will follow up all of these leads to make sure they have received the book and to politely hassle them to read it, and do so in a way that doesn't elicit a 'Will you please fuck off' from the recipient. Recipients spend a fair bit of their time avoiding emails and calls from publicity people.

So far, so good, but now I want to throw in a bit of a reality check and also a rather clunky analogy for you. (No need to thank me.)

Imagine the publicity person who is handling your book is sitting in front of a conveyor belt. The conveyor belt is constantly in motion while they stay in a fixed position. On the conveyor belt, in chronological order of publication, are all the books that publisher has coming out in the year ahead. They join the conveyor belt when they are signed and

---

3   Often, publishers produce a short print run of very early copies, sometimes before the final text has been proofread, purely for this purpose. These are variously known as advance reading copies, galleys, proof copies, galley proofs and probably a few other names that all mean the same thing.

drop off the end a few weeks after they arrive in bookshops.

Got that in your head? Good.

Now, because the publicity person is in a fixed position, only a certain number of books are in their eyeline at any one time. Books start to appear a few months before publication. At this point they can make tentative plans. As the book gets closer to publication, and within arm's reach, they can send out advance reading copies and press releases. When the book is bang in front of them they can chase up reviews, get the author interviewed, chase all the publicity they can. But just a few weeks after publication the book drops off the end and they have to focus their attention on the books coming at them from the other side.

And, for most authors, that is pretty much it. You will get publicity support from your publisher for a couple of months around publication but, unless your book really takes off and is a massive hit deserving of further promotion, there simply are not the resources to keep going beyond that point. This comes as a surprise to many, but will no longer come as a surprise to you.

Although on one level this sort of makes sense – publishers cannot spend a year promoting each and every book, media are interested in new titles, not titles that are a few months old, resources are finite – it also ignores the way the world of readers has changed in recent years. Largely due to social media, word-of-mouth is now a far more powerful force in book sales, and it often doesn't kick in until a book has been published for a while. To take one example, *The Corner Shop in Cockleberry Bay*, by Nicola May, became the bestselling book in the Amazon UK Kindle charts one full year after publication, selling thousands upon thousands of copies every single day. Because it was a self-published book, Nicola had been able to plug away at publicity for many months. If it had been published traditionally, the publicity would have ended after just a few weeks and it probably would not have enjoyed the significant success that it did – or gone on to spawn bestselling sequels.

Just because a particular way of working is traditional, or practical, or is 'just the way things are done', does not mean it is the most effective.

In summary, you are unlikely to have much, if any, marketing activity for your book. You will almost certainly receive publicity support, and it could be very effective, but it is likely to be limited to the month or so on either side of your publication date.

Printing and distribution

Although retailers like to know about books several months before they are published, they (rather annoyingly) tend only to confirm their orders quite late in the day. Therefore, final copies of a book are often not printed until shortly before official publication date.

The vast majority of publishers, quite possibly all of them these days, have their books printed by a third party, and most countries have a small number of specialist book printers who are used for this purpose. Books are not always printed in their country of origin, though. A standard book, containing just text, will usually be printed in the same country as it is being published because mono-printing (as black text and illustrations on a white page is known in the trade) is the cheapest option and there isn't much price difference from one place to another. A typical lead-time for such a printing job would be a couple of weeks, depending on how many other books the printer has on their schedule.

Colour printing, however, is a whole different thing and can be obtained for a far lower price in the Far East, especially China and Hong Hong. So books that contain lots of colour images, such as cookbooks or children's picture books, are often printed on the other side of the world and then, to keep costs low, shipped over on, well, a ship. So, although a colour book can often be printed within a couple of weeks, it may take two to three months to actually arrive in the publisher's warehouse because ships don't travel as fast as planes.

In terms of the actual printing process itself, it is, as you might expect, largely computerised these days. The publisher sends over electronic files containing the cover and text as well as specifications for type of paper[4] and any cover finishes[5]. The printer checks these over and then schedules the printing, partly based on the urgency of the job but also

---

4   Despite what certain idiots might believe or say, we are actually in the midst of a climate crisis so most of the paper used in printing books these days comes from certifiable and sustainable sources, which is a good thing.

5   Pick up a few random books from your shelves and you will probably find author names or book titles that are de-bossed (raised up and bumpy), or certain features of the cover might have a shiny finish, known as spot-varnish, or some metallic foiling. Or some combination of the above. These are seen to enhance the design, make the book look a bit more fancy, but they all cost more money so tend to be used sparingly, and often just on the first print run of a book.

on how best to make use of their facilities and paper stock. Much better to print four different books in a row when they all use the same paper, for example.

And then, finally, many months, often more than a year after you signed your book contract, an actual printed copy of your book comes off the press.

Finished books are then sent to a warehouse (some big publishers have their own warehouses but most use third-party companies that specialise in book distribution) where they should ideally arrive four to six weeks ahead of publication date so that stock can be logged in, allocated a space and scheduled for shipping. Then, shortly before official publication date, copies are sent out to the bookshops and other retailers who have placed orders. The remaining stock sits in the warehouse in the hope of new orders and reorders coming in.

The printing and distribution of books are two of the big costs that a publisher has to account for when publishing a book. With printing, they pay a unit price per copy, partly based on the number of pages but also on the number of copies that are printed. So, for example, if my publisher chose to print 1,000 copies of this book they will have paid perhaps as much as £1.50 per copy. If they printed 3,000 it would have been around 75p per copy. 10,000 would be closer to 40p per copy. So, as you can see, convincing retailers to buy lots of your book can be hugely beneficial when it comes to print costs.

Retailers

Every book is allocated an official publication date and although this will be a very important date for the author, with launch parties organised and emails to all and sundry telling them when the book will be available in bookshops, hardly anyone within the industry will give a shit about it. Apart from a very few strictly embargoed titles, such as a new George RR Martin novel or yet another *Harry Potter* spin-off, most books arrive in bookshops a week or two before publication and are put out on sale when they arrive, limping out there in dribs and drabs. Put simply, your debut novel is not really a big deal to the Saturday lad in Waterstones who has been told to stick it on the shelves. It is just another book among many. And, of course, when it comes to copies sent to an Amazon warehouse it is even more anonymous, sitting somewhere in a big hangar until an order is received and a robot, or poorly-paid worker, has to find it and pop it in a cardboard box.

Sorry about that, but it's true.

Hopefully your book will, as we have previously discussed, get some good publicity and review coverage, and people will start buying it and reading it and telling everyone else how wonderful it is. That means lots of copies will be selling and the various book retailers will be ordering more stock from the warehouse, and then selling it, and so on and so forth. I go into the retail model in more detail later in the book if you really want to get stuck into the nitty gritty.

Whatever the sales, though, your book is a real actual thing that people can buy from bookshops and write reviews about on GoodReads and Amazon and take fancy staged photos of for Instagram. It has been quite the journey. But it isn't quite over yet.

What happens next?

Ahh, what a question. No two books have identical journeys, of course, but there are a few typical routes that many follow. Here are some of them.

For a small number of books, the bestseller charts will beckon. Luck, timing, talent and the appetite of readers will coincide beautifully, and hundreds of thousands of copies will sell. A bestselling book in one country will usually translate (pun noted, but not intended) to book deals being made in other countries and other languages. You will make some decent money and there will be a strong desire for more books from you. No pressure. A big bestseller will probably remain in demand in bookshops for many years to come.

You can sell tens of thousands across a year or two and never make the *Sunday Times* or *New York Times* bestseller lists. Tens of thousands is a lot of books and certainly enough to prompt international interest, and for your publisher to want to sign you up for another book or two. Nice work. You can certainly expect to see your book on the shelves of your favourite bookshop for the next year or so, but beyond that it will depend on ongoing sales or how your next books have performed.

Most books will sell sort of OK. A few thousand or so. No shame in that at all. If someone had told you when you were still writing your book that 3,000 people would pay good money to read it you would probably have been pretty pleased. Sure, you would have preferred it to be 300,000, but 3,000 is still a lot of people. Whether it is enough to warrant a deal for a second book from your publisher will depend on their original expectations. And don't expect to see your book in every bookshop in the land even around publication, let alone months or years later.

Sadly some books do flop, tank, fail, and many supposed failures really are great books. Some of my favourite books of the past twenty years, books I still recommend to others and champion left, right and centre, failed to sell in any great numbers. It happens to a lot of authors and is one of the hazards of the industry. Not every book will be a success. Of course, if your book fails to sell well then it will be harder to get a deal for your next book, but not impossible.

If, after a year or more, sales of a book have slowed down considerably, and the publisher has lots of stock left, then other methods of handling the surplus copies will be explored. Remainder sales are where a publisher sells excess stock to a company that specialises in selling books cheap, sometimes on Amazon Marketplace, or in specialist discount stores. These sales will be at a massively reduced price but will at least make a little money. If this isn't possible then publishers may decide to pulp the books. This is where the cost of keeping them in the warehouse outweighs the income received from selling them, and they are effectively sent off to be destroyed and recycled. Not nice, but it makes financial sense. In both of these scenarios, it is traditional for the author to be offered copies at a greatly reduced price.

However, books will stay available in bookshops, with publishers reprinting copies when stocks are getting low, for as long as there is a demand for them. But demand will drop off for all books – even *Harry Potter* doesn't sell as much now as it did in the 2000s – and if it falls below a point where a reprint is not financially viable then it can become what is known as 'out of print', with no new copies being made. Readers can still pick up the remaining copies from bookshops, or second-hand copies from Amazon or charity shops or wherever, but to all intents and purposes stock is allowed to run out and the book is no longer commercially available. At this point, authors can ask for the rights to revert back to them and do with those rights what they will. Nowadays, many authors self-publish reissues of their own books, and often do very nicely from it.

Suffice to say, most books have a finite life span in the frontline of the book world. There are so many books published every year that there simply isn't room for them all in bookshops, so it is inevitable, and necessary, for older books to make way for the new. Your time in the limelight may be relatively short, so make the most of it.

And here ends the journey of your book, from keyboard to bookshop, and beyond. Whether its ultimate fate is as an international bestseller or as a pulp used to build roads[6], it will, for a while, have been a real, proper, printed book – and that is a wonderful thing to have happened.

---

6   The M6 toll road in the UK is built upon pulped copies of Mills & Boon romances.

2

A Writer's Guide to Publishing Models

As part of my mission (which is probably too grand a word) to demystify the publishing world for you, this chapter will look at the various models and business practices that exist within it. All of them ultimately result in a book being sold to a reader but that outcome can be approached in a number of different ways, and the model or models you end up being part of can significantly affect your experience as an author. Here, then, is a simple guide to how it all works.

The traditional model

For decades, perhaps even centuries, there has been one prevalent model in the publishing industry, and it is the one that all major publishers adhere to, so I feel comfortable describing it as the traditional model.

This is how it works.

An author submits their book to an agent and, for the sake of this example, let's assume the submission is successful and the agent agrees to represent the author.

The agent then submits the book to publishers.

If the agent finds a publisher that wants the book, that publisher offers an amount of money as an advance. This is, as the name suggests, an advance payment, in this case against future royalties.

The publisher goes away and does everything that needs doing to produce the book, and they pay all the costs of this production.

The publisher then attempts to sell as many copies of the book as they can, through bookshops and online sales. The author is entitled to a percentage of the revenue, known as a royalty, but the publisher keeps all the proceeds from the book until the advance has been recouped.

Once the book has sold enough copies to make back the advance, the author will receive royalties on all further sales.

For donkey's years this is how the vast majority of books have been acquired and published. And like any long-established practice, it has its good points and its bad points.

PROS

- Because this has been the dominant model for so long, the publishing industry is essentially built around it. Almost every aspect of how a book is published has some link to this way of doing things and this means authors and books that follow this model have, by default, a better chance of 'fitting in' to the system.

- And it works, most of the time. We'll come to the drawbacks in a moment but, by and large, this is a successful system that generates profit for all parties when a book sells well.

- One big advantage for authors is that they get a payment upfront. It may not always be a large payment, but it is something, and when you consider that it may be 12 to 18 months between signing a contract and the first physical copy being sold, it is clearly a good thing to have some sort of money in the bank as early in that process as possible.

CONS

- You probably won't be able to get anyone to admit it, but this is a model based on guesswork. No one really knows how many copies a book is going to sell, so deciding upon an advance is a bit of a punt. Sure, the people in suits with calculators who manage the money will have spreadsheets and systems to try to make it slightly more scientific, but it is bloody hard to predict what a book will sell at some point in the future when you don't even have a cover and only the acquiring editor has read it. As a result, publishers often get the size of the advance wrong.

- And this leads to a situation known as an unrecouped advance, where the author never actually sells enough books to make their advance back, so the advance is the only payment they ever receive. If the advance was of sufficient size you may not think this matters too much, but it does have knock-on effects. It means that publishers have to write off big pots of money they will never make back, and this takes money out of the industry that could have been spent on other authors. It can also effectively stifle an author's career. The book world is littered with writers who received big advances for their first book, only for that book not to sell as well as hoped, and they are then seen as something of a failure, which is daft as many of these 'failures' will have sold tens of thousands of copies.

- Having said that, huge advances are rarer these days and average advance amounts have decreased enormously. If an author gets more than £5,000 then they have done pretty well. And although that is not an amount of money to be sniffed at, it isn't a life-changing sum for most people, so the benefit of being paid some or all of this upfront is nowhere near as great as with a £50,000 or £100,000 advance. Obviously.

- The traditional model also keeps the author at arm's length from the reader, the person actually buying and reading the book. Author deals with agent, agent deals with editor, editor deals with publishing colleagues, the sales team deals with the booksellers, and the booksellers have the relationship with the readers. So what's that? Five times removed? Sure, authors can interact with readers through social media and book events but the actual model being used to publish the books keeps a big distance between them.

- And, finally, as many readers of this book will be only too well aware, this is a very difficult model to break into. I make part of my living by giving classes and workshops on how to improve your chances of getting an agent, and I certainly wouldn't be able to charge for tickets if this were an easy thing to do. Most publishers will not accept unsolicited manuscripts, so authors have to find an agent, and that is a notoriously painful and difficult process.

Whatever its pros and cons, it is well worth familiarising yourself with this model as it is the one that most of you will be dealing with in your life as a writer.

Small and independent publishers

One of the wonderful things about the book world in recent decades is the rise of the small publisher – independent companies that often focus on one specific area of literature and then publish it with skill and dexterity. They do, of course, need to fit into the overall industry in order to survive. They tend therefore to follow the traditional model previously outlined, but with a few small tweaks.

And these tweaks are largely financial. Advances tend to be smaller – £1,000 would not be uncommon – and sometimes there is no advance at all. This is largely because small publishers don't have lots of money, and they will be taking on all the costs of producing the book, so there is, to be honest, little sense in gambling with big advances.

Agents, understandably, prioritise the publishers who will pay the most money, so the smaller indies often don't see a manuscript until it has been rejected by the bigger ones. As a result, they can be more open to unsolicited manuscripts, which means authors without agents actually get a look-in. They are also more likely to take a risk with an unknown author.

In recent years, indies have started to explore some of the alternative publishing models I will outline in the following pages, but for now let's look at the benefits and drawbacks of small publishers that stick to the traditional way of doing things.

PROS

- Smaller publishers will publish fewer books than the big guys, so an author is a bigger fish in a smaller pond. There is less chance of being lost in the big corporate machine. Ask anyone, in any role, at a small press what books they are publishing this year and they'll be able to excitedly reel off a list of authors and titles and tell you all about them. The same won't always happen with someone at a big publishing house, not because they aren't interested but simply because there are so many books being published and they can't keep track of them all.

- Indies can be more nimble, more creative, needing fewer people to sign off cover designs or marketing plans or the like. You also tend to find they are far less at the mercy of the sales department.
- And one good thing about a low advance is that it is much easier to recoup, with authors often earning actual royalties within the first year of publication.

CONS

- Smaller publishers tend to be smaller in every respect, and that includes the size of marketing budgets and their overall clout within the industry. This is often the root of their exciting creativity, but it can also be limiting and restricting when it comes to getting space in newspaper review pages and on the shelves of bookshops.
- It can be hard to make a living on a £1,000 advance and modest book sales. There are very few authors published by small publishers who make their entire living that way.

I have worked for a massive publisher and also a few small indies and while the massive one had major economies of scale and significant influence with book retailers, it was hard to make any individual title stand out from the crowd. The indies were much more title-focused, which is great, but with a smaller staff and smaller budgets any problems – personality conflicts, poor sales performance, higher costs – have greater negative impact and are harder to absorb.

Profit share

A model that is becoming increasingly popular in publishing, especially with smaller publishers, is profit share. It can sound a bit scary at first, and perhaps a little off-putting, but it does have a lot going for it and it may be something you are faced with and need to consider.

In this way of doing things, the author receives no advance and the publisher pays the entire costs of production. These costs are totted up and recorded and the author receives no payment at all until they are recouped. But once the sales revenue from the book exceeds the costs, you have a profit and, with profit share, that surplus is usually split 50/50 between author and publisher.

So if your book costs the publisher £6000 to create, print and sell, and they are making £2 in revenue from every copy sold (which would be typical on a £7.99 paperback, allowing for discount and costs), then once they have sold 3,000 copies the book could well be in profit, and from that point on the profit will be shared between you.

I am a big fan of this model and, in fact, my own deal for this book is profit share. So if enough of you buy copies I should be able to afford plenty of Tunnock's Caramel Wafers (my snack of choice) in the years ahead. It is less popular with agents, though, as 15% of a zero advance isn't going to keep them in the more deluxe biscuits they tend to eat.

PROS

- The fact that publishers don't have to shell out an advance, years before they are likely to recoup it, allows them to take a few more risks. But aren't risks, well, more risky? They sure are, but if their willingness to take a risk means they are prepared to publish your book, then you may feel it is more than worth it.

- When done well, this can be a straightforward and transparent way to do business. Removing all the high discount clauses (I cover these in 'The Mathematics of Publishing' chapter) and replacing them with a simple split of profits is easier to manage and understand.

- It can end up far more profitable for authors if a book sells well.

- It is an excellent model when it comes to ebooks, which have none of the printing, distribution and returns costs of print editions. An ebook that sells thousands of copies can make a lot of money for the author with a profit share deal.

- This sort of model can encourage a more collaborative relationship between author and publisher, with the author often being consulted far more closely on aspects such as cover and text design as well as marketing and publicity.

CONS

- Well, the most obvious one is that some books never make a profit and, when that happens, the author makes no money out of the book. The fact that there is a physical book available in bookshops may be some consolation but it would be nice to have something in the bank to show for it.

- The contract needs to be transparent and fair in order for this to work. You may have heard of dodgy movie deals where an actor is offered a percentage of net profits on a film, with the film then taking hundreds of millions of dollars at the box office yet, seemingly, never making an actual profit due to creative accounting. Some people are therefore wary of this sort of deal and it requires a level of trust that many are not prepared to offer. However, as long as you are clear what is considered a cost then you should not face any nasty surprises.

- This model is much harder to make work when it comes to books with high production costs. Photography books, cookery books – anything with lots of pictures and fancy design, anything to be printed in colour, basically – can cost well over £10,000 to produce. OK, so the RRP is often higher to make up for this but it can still be tough to make a profit.

- You may have to wait some time before you actually receive any money. If you sign a contract in January of one year, your book may not appear till March of the next year, and it may take another year for the book to make a profit, so your first royalties could be more than two years away.

A few words about...

Do writers need agents, or should they bypass them and go straight to a publisher instead? After all, why pay someone 15% of your earnings if you can do the work yourself? These are reasonable questions, so let me provide you with reasonable answers.

If you decide to self-publish then you don't need an agent, and an agent is unlikely to want to sign you up anyway. Should you go on to enjoy massive success as a self-published author then agents might be interested, and you may be in more need of someone to help manage your affairs, but that is not something you need to concern yourself with to start with. No agent required. Move on.

Conversely, if you really want to be published by a major publishing house then you have no choice but to secure an agent. Big publishers don't welcome unsolicited manuscripts so you have no way of getting your work to them without the help of an agent. If, for you, it is Penguin Books or nothing then you need to get submitting to agents who can put your magnum opus in front of editors at Penguin.

But now we come to the inevitable grey area. Medium- and small-sized publishers, who are often independent with small teams of staff, tend to be more open to unsolicited manuscripts and don't expect all their authors to have agents. So there is nothing to stop you submitting direct without any need to bother with an agent at all and, in most cases, the fact that you don't have an agent will not hinder your chances of being published.

However, you will be on your own when it comes to negotiating the deal, navigating the contract, trying to influence things such as publication date, having a say in cover design, resolving any problems that crop up, and you will probably be doing so with no prior knowledge of the way the publishing world works (even if this book has helped you learn the basics).

As mentioned later in this chapter on publishing models, agents come into their own when it comes to rights. Their ability to sell UK & Commonwealth, US, translation and audiobook rights to different companies is a great way of boosting your income, and few indie publishers are in a position to do this quite as effectively.

I know of several authors who have started out by getting their own deal with a small publisher, enjoyed reasonable success, and then gone on to secure an agent on the back of that. This is certainly a viable route, one you may wish to consider if your attempts to secure an agent don't work out.

As with many questions, the answer to whether or not you should get an agent is a big fat IT DEPENDS, but I would recommend attempting to get yourself an agent initially and then perhaps reviewing your strategy over time.

...agents and publishers

Crowdfunding

It seems as if everything is being crowdfunded these days: movies, albums, restaurants, computer games, all manner of weird and wonderful inventions. I have even helped to fund a butter knife, of all things. There are numerous crowdfunding websites out there, some with a wide range of projects on offer and others that specialise in a certain subject, and, of course, there are some that focus purely on books.

I can only see this style of publishing model increasing in the years ahead, so even if you are not considering it at the moment it would be worth wrapping your head around it for future reference.

Essentially this model turns the funding side of things upside down. In the other models we have looked at, the publisher has to pay all the costs of the book – advance, editorial, design, production, sales, marketing, distribution – before it has sold a single copy. Nearly all of the financial risk is upfront and readers do not get involved until the book arrives in bookshops or online.

But with crowdfunding, readers get involved much earlier in the process and their money covers most of the costs before a single copy is printed, effectively removing much of the risk.

Here's how it works.

A budget is created for the book. This would take into account the cost of producing the book, from editorial right up to delivery to readers. The total amount becomes the target that needs to be raised by the publisher, or author, depending on who has set up the project.

A list of rewards is then drawn up. This comprises a wide, and often highly imaginative, array of items. The idea is to offer the reader a bunch of stuff above and beyond just a copy of the book, things they can only get if they help to crowdfund the project. So, you may have a copy of the paperback book for £10, a signed copy for £15, dinner with the author for £50, signed limited edition cover art for £75 or whatever. The sky's the limit, really. Sometimes authors will offer a Patron level, costing upwards of £1,000, which will get a person's name in a special dedication in the front of the book. Having a character named after you is also quite a popular choice. The cost of fulfilling these rewards is built into the budget.

An appeal for funds is then made direct to readers. This is often a combination of a promotional video, a social-media campaign, an email mail-out and personal approaches, all of which direct people to a web page, which is usually part of a larger crowdfunding site.

When readers reach the site, they pick a reward and pledge for it. When enough people have pledged for the project, and the target is hit, the book can then be put into production and the rewards delivered. If the project has been set up by the author themselves, on a platform such as Kickstarter, they then need to go away and pay editors and designers and printers to get the book made. If a publisher is behind it, they will handle that stuff. In both instances, the crowdfunded money is used to cover the costs.

If a book doesn't hit its target then supporters get their money back.

If a book significantly over-funds, it is clearly in profit before it is even made, which is great. If the author has organised the crowdfunding themselves, all that profit goes to them. If they have teamed up with a publisher, it is usually split 50/50.

PROS

- Crowdfunding removes almost all the risk from publishing. Apart from the costs of recording a promotional video and setting up the initial project page, nothing else needs to be spent until the money is raised to cover it.
- It is a publishing model that brings author and reader much closer together[7], often literally. Whether it be the initial appeal for pledges via social media or sitting down for dinner with each other, there is far more contact between the two.
- It is often a great deal for the reader, offering them rewards that they would rarely, if ever, be able to get from a bookshop.
- It can be hugely profitable. A quick browse of some book projects on crowdfunding sites will find many that are thousands, and even tens of thousands, of pounds over their targets.

---

7   One of my lovely beta readers, Rebecca, made this note here: 'I don't know why it is a pro to bring reader and author closer together. I shall want my readers to stay the fuck away.' Which I am sharing with you for reasons of balance.

CONS

- This is not a model that is suitable for everyone. It takes a certain type of person, quite a thick-skinned one, to approach friends, acquaintances and strangers and ask them to pay in advance for a book that doesn't exist yet. And it requires an even bolder person to keep going back to people until they cough up.
- The whole process involves a lot of networking, and it is a great deal easier if you already have a network – e.g. Twitter followers, YouTube subscribers – to tap into and motivate. It doesn't have to be a huge network, as long as they are engaged and prepared to invest, but the truth is that few people have that sort of network available.
- The failure rate is pretty high. 30-40% of crowdfunding projects will never hit their targets.
- There can be a long wait for supporters. You could pledge for a book in its first day of funding, it then takes six months to fund, another year to go through the production schedule. It could be two years or more between initial payment and book delivery. It is not unheard of for people to have completely forgotten they have pledged for a book by the time it arrives. I know I have.
- And all of this effort just produces books for your supporters. There is no route to bookshops if you personally crowdfund your book. The specialist crowdfunding publishers do usually have a route to bookshops, but that is not the case for individual authors.

My advice to anyone considering crowdfunding is to spend time on the various websites available and also, if possible, support a project or two to see how they work from the supporter's perspective. There are lots of How To guides online, and on the crowdfunding websites themselves, which offer tips and guidance for this type of publishing, so avail yourselves of those. Do your research.

Digital-only publishers

In recent years a new generation of publishers has emerged that don't bother with printing books or selling their wares in bookshops at all. The rise of the ebook has meant that there is a viable business model in digital-only publishing, and it is a model that avoids many of the hefty costs of more traditional ones.

Digital-only publishers still spend money on editing and cover design, and often have strong online marketing and publicity strategies, but obviously they are not spending a penny on printing or distribution. As a result they can offer higher royalties to authors.

A typical ebook royalty is 25% of net receipts if an author is published via the traditional model, so that is 25% of all revenue received by the publisher from Amazon, Kobo, Apple and other ebook retailers. A digital-only publisher will often offer 50% or above.

Genres that work particularly well as ebooks include crime, science fiction, fantasy, thrillers, romance, romantic comedies and erotica. But literary fiction, poetry, and most scholarly non-fiction can struggle on the format.

PROS

- The higher royalty is a clear winner, and many authors have made a considerable living from ebook sales at this sort of royalty level.
- Publishers can produce books far more quickly, just a few months in some cases, rather than the 12-18 months that the traditional model requires.
- Digital-only publishers are far more likely to take a punt on a new author and welcome unsolicited manuscripts.

CONS

- Many authors still only feel they have truly made it if they have a print edition on sale in bookshops, and that certainly is not the case with this model.
- Nor will you see your book reviewed in the newspaper review pages. They don't review books unless they are available in print editions.
- It can be hard for a new ebook to be discovered by readers among the many thousands of self-published and traditionally published titles that appear each week. Customers don't browse ebooks in the way they do print books in a bookshop.

Self-publishing

In the not too distant past, self-publishing was seen as a version of vanity publishing (more on which shortly) and largely frowned upon by the industry – agents, publishers, reviewers and booksellers alike. But, my word, how things have changed, and primarily down to everyone's favourite evil retail empire, Amazon.

As we have seen, the traditional publishing model is hard to break into because it is managed and overseen by a series of gatekeepers. For your book to be published it has to be deemed 'good enough' by an agent, and then by a publisher, meaning that agents and editors are the arbiters of taste and quality.

When Amazon made it free, and easy, to publish your own books and sell them on its site, the gates were suddenly wide open. And what happened is that lots of shitty books with their even more shitty covers flooded the market. These, by and large, failed to sell. But there were also lots of very good, and even great, books published, and they were embraced by eager readers. Many authors realised they were able to find an audience and make a decent living from self-publishing their books, even if no newspaper reviewed them and no bookshop stocked them.

It was a seismic shift for the industry.

With self-publishing, as the name suggests, the author organises everything themselves. They write the book, obviously, but they also get it edited, get the cover and text designed, and arrange printing, sales and distribution. Everything is down to them.

In some cases, although I would never advise this, the author literally does everything, taking on each task themselves, but the chances that you are some literary version of Prince, highly skilled in numerous disciplines, are slim. I doubt you are as good at writing as you are at editing or cover design and so on.

More sensible authors will farm out each task to an expert, becoming more of a project manager, pulling everything together to ensure the final book is produced to a high standard.

PROS

- The author is in control and has final say on all aspects of the book.
- No need to plug into an antiquated and convoluted traditional model. No need to wait for months to find an agent. You can just get on with it.
- The author receives all the revenue from sales and they are paid monthly. No 7.5% royalty paid twice a year with this model.

CONS

- That shift from author to publisher is a big one. This is a huge task. It is a bit like building a house and managing it all yourself, rather than bringing in an architect or project manager to deal with much of it for you.
- And of course 100% of the costs and 100% of the risk lies with the author. You could end up pissing away

thousands of pounds on this project, and getting very little back in return.

- Although it is simple enough to publish an ebook and put it for sale on Amazon, it is much harder to produce a print edition and even harder to convince bookshops to stock it.

- And then we have sales and marketing. The effort expended by self-publishers in spreading the word, and flogging their books, is often greater than in writing and publishing the bloody things. I have friends who have enjoyed considerable success through self-publishing and all of them, bar none, have said at one time or another: 'I wish I had more time to write.'

- Finally, not too put too fine a point on it, many self-published authors aren't very good at it, or aren't very good at key aspects of the process. You might have written a great crime novel, and then slapped a crap cover on it, thereby dooming your work of genius to ridicule and obscurity. You may have a decent story on your hands but you have skipped the copyedit to save money and now you have a book out there that is full of grammatical errors.

Usually I advise authors to at least try the traditional route, or one of its modern adaptations, before self-publishing. You might as well give it a shot before taking on the huge task of doing it all yourself.

Joint venture

You won't come across this somewhat niche model all that often, but I wanted to mention it just in case you do as there are good examples and bad examples out there, and I am keen that you are able to tell them apart.

The principle of a joint venture is that both publisher and author contribute to the costs of production, venturing into it jointly, so to speak.

With what I would consider a 'good' version of this model, the author's level of reward is commensurate with the level of investment. So if an author contributes 30% of the costs, they receive 30% of the revenue. And by revenue I mean *all* income, not a royalty. Every £10 the publisher receives in sales, the author gets £3. In such a version both publisher and author are sharing risk and sharing potential rewards.

'Bad' versions would include those that offer the author nothing above and beyond a traditional royalty deal. In such a version, the author and publisher are sharing risk but the author is not receiving a fair share of the potential rewards.

PROS

- If the publisher has established sales and distribution channels, then this can be an effective way for an author with some spare funds to help bring a book to market.
- It can be particularly attractive to authors who have a decent pile of savings and/or have a proven audience for their book. For example, if you are a motivational

speaker and able to sell books at your events, but want a professional publisher to produce the book and sell it in bookshops, then this could be more attractive than self-publishing. You know you'll sell hundreds or thousands of books a year, and feel a return is guaranteed, and you have some funds to help make it happen.

CONS

- There is absolutely no guarantee of a return.
- This sort of arrangement is often viewed as analogous to vanity publishing and some newspapers, prizes and shops may not consider featuring a book published via this model. This is one of the reasons publishers often keep quiet about it.

Vanity publishing

Vanity publishing has long been the scourge of the industry. It has been frowned upon, disapproved of and ridiculed for decades, if not centuries. I am here to tell you that it is not *all* bad.

But first, an explanation. Vanity publishing, as the name unsubtly suggests, is where an author pays to get their book published. Typically, this would be a few thousand pounds and would cover all the costs of production and printing, the final price determined by how many copies get printed.

The key thing to note with vanity publishing is that the end product, the published book, is not going to be stocked in bookshops. It will be available at Amazon and other online retailers as long as the book has an ISBN, and most vanity publishers will offer that as part of the package. It could also be ordered in by bookshops if someone wanted it, even if it won't sit on their shelves as a regular stock item, but it won't be actively sold to shops and the vast majority won't have it on their shelves.

So if you have paid £5,000 to have your book edited, designed and 500 copies printed, expecting it to be on sale in your local Waterstones, then you are going to be very disappointed, and your garage is going to be full of books for many years to come.

But here is where I think vanity publishing has a place: if you are a jolly old granddad who wants to write his life story and have 20 copies printed for friends and family, this sort of model will probably suit you just fine.

PROS

- There is no submissions process, no convoluted production, marketing and sales models to navigate – you just pay the fee and your book is created.

CONS

- There is no direct or obvious route to market for the book you have paid to publish.

If you are seriously considering this route then just make sure you understand how much it is going to cost you and what you will get out of it at the end.

The agent model

Now to look at a few models that aren't directly linked to the actual publishing of books. As you will have seen, many of the routes to publication involve having an agent, and I will be covering the best strategies to adopt for finding an agent later on in the book, but while we are discussing models it would seem prudent to be familiar with how agents work and operate.

Agents, like editors and publishers, can be part of companies both big and small. Some agencies are huge, with offices all over the world, others are tiny, with just a few employees. The size of the company matters a lot less than the passions, skills and expertise of the individual agents.

When an agent signs an author, they agree that the agent will act as the author's representative – a business manager, if you will. A good agent will handle all the author's interests when it comes to writing and writing-related matters.

The agent will usually also get involved in editing the author's work, often the first professional to get stuck into the manuscript. They will help knock the book into shape and get it ready to submit to publishers.

They will then attempt to 'sell' the book to publishers, and this will usually mean separating out the different rights to the book and selling them individually. So they could sell UK & Commonwealth print and ebook rights to one publisher, but sell the US rights to a different one, receiving an advance for each. Likewise, they could sell translation rights to several publishers in a variety of countries. And they could also sell audiobook rights and film or television rights separately as well.

As you can see, this could be a lucrative way of doing things. Rather than getting one advance from one publisher, the author could get three, seven, ten, twenty, or more, different advances for the same book, depending on how successful the agent has been.

The agent will handle all the boring/scary/complicated stuff such as financial negotiations, contracts etc. An agent allows the author to concentrate as much as possible on the writing.

For all of this work and effort, the agent will typically take a 15% commission on all the revenue they generate for you. They receive all the money for your books, take off their 15%, and then pass on the rest.

The relationship between agent and author, although initially a business one, can often develop into a genuine friendship, especially when they have been working together for several years. Because of this, authors often follow their agents when the latter move from one company to another.

PROS

- It can be wonderful to have someone handle all this stuff so that you don't have to.
- As agents increasingly become the first editors for a book, they also become a vital part of the writing, or re-writing, process for authors. Their input is hugely valuable.
- The ability for an agent to split and sell rights separately, something most authors have no way of doing

themselves, can make a notable difference to the income an author receives.

- An author's relationship with their agent is often the longest relationship they have in their writing lives. They may move publishing house, they may have different editors, but many have the same agent forever.

CONS

- Agents tend to represent a number of different authors, so you could be one of many, and their focus can shift depending on which of their authors are doing what at any particular time. If you have just sent them the manuscript for your second book at the same time as their big superstar author has a new bestseller hitting the bookshops, then you may feel a little neglected.

- Also, think about it, if you are an agent making 15% on all the revenue you generate, and one of your authors sells a million copies a year and another sells 5,000, which author's emails are you going to reply to straight away and which one may have to wait a day or two for a response? I know of many authors who have found an agent, to their great joy, only to experience moderate sales and find that their agent is no longer as attentive as they once were. When that happens, of course, you are free to move to a different agent, if you can find one.

I usually advise authors to try to get an agent if at all possible, as the pros of having one far outweigh any potential cons. Just having a person who can deal with contracts and any publishing disputes is hugely beneficial.

The retail model

I was head of buying for the Waterstones book chain in the UK for several years, so retail was my life for quite some time, and I often find myself surprised by how many authors are ignorant of, or have misconceptions about, the way this side of the business works. I think it helps if authors understand the retail model so I wanted to explore it in this chapter.

All book retailers, whether big corporate chains or small individual independents, will have new and forthcoming books presented to them by publishers on a regular basis. They need to decide which ones to stock, and in what sort of quantity, alongside all the books they already have on their shelves.

The nature of these presentations will differ quite widely. When I was in charge of the new-title buying team at Waterstones we would meet with the bigger publishers two or three times a year to go through the highlights of their future publishing plans. So we might meet with HarperCollins in the spring and be shown the key books they were publishing in autumn, then meet again in summer to go through their winter titles. These were often fancy presentations with a number of attendees and did a good job of making us aware of the titles they had big plans for in the months ahead.

Then, every month, the HarperCollins sales director would pop into our office and present more detailed information on the books coming out in 2-3 months' time. This is where orders, deals and promotional plans would be discussed.

Indie publishers who sold a fair few books in our stores would also get access to the buying team but less regularly, maybe twice a year. Publishers smaller than this may not get to see us in person but would send us information instead. And, of course, we would receive advance reading copies galore.

All of the information for a particular month's new books would be reviewed by the buying team, who would place orders for the stores.

That's how it works with the retail chains and supermarkets, with some variations. Independent bookshops may get invited to big sales presentations once a year or so, but the day-to-day sales decisions are usually taken by the manager of the shop in consultation with sales reps from the companies, or salespeople from the wholesalers (more on them to come). These discussions may be had over the counter, or the phone, or via email, but follow the same basic premise: publisher presents books and bookseller decides which ones to buy and how many.

As with any aspect of retail the supplier (publisher) sells products (books) to their client (bookshop) with some sort of agreed deal. This usually involves a level of discount, an approved level of returns and sometimes some marketing spend.

I cover much of the financial aspect of this in 'The Mathematics of Publishing' chapter but should probably repeat some of the key points here. Every book in the UK, and in most other counties, has an RRP (recommended retail price) printed on the cover. The publisher offers the retailer discount from that RRP. So if HarperCollins offers

Waterstones 60% discount on an £8.99 paperback then Waterstones are paying £3.59 per copy. They can then sell it at any price up to and including £8.99 and make whatever profit that delivers.

The same principle applies to all publisher-to-bookshop sales but, as you might expect, the bigger retailers tend to buy more copies and thus get bigger discounts. That's capitalism for you. These discounts could range from 35% for small independent bookshops to 70%+ for bigger chains, supermarkets and Amazon.

But that's not all. Most books sold to retailers by publishers are sold on a sale-or-return basis. This means that bookshops can send back any unsold stock, usually after an agreed period (typically between three and 18 months following receipt). This is why accounting for returns is so difficult for publishers, as they cannot be sure when they will receive them – hence the returns provision in most author royalty statements. This is an amount held back to cover potential future returns. On average, around 20% of all books sold to bookshops come back to publishers in the end.

And there is still more. Sometimes, mainly with the biggest retailers, publishers will also pay a marketing contribution. This is a fee that they pay in order to be part of a promotion. For example, any book you see in the chart at your local WH Smith will have been subject to a fee of anywhere between a few hundred pounds and a couple of thousand. It is important to stress that publishers can't just pay the money and put any old shit in there, the books have to be selected by the retailers first, but that doesn't stop this from being a controversial part of the model. However, the number one position in the book chart in 1,000+ branches of a major book retailer across the country is prime retail space and has value. Even if it does seem unfair.

I have gone on a bit here but I want you to understand how the system operates and to give you an idea as to quite how hard it is to get a book stocked by a bookshop, big or small. Thousands of books are published every month, and each one has to jump through all manner of hoops before it stands a chance of ending up on the shelves of a bookshop.

PROS

- Hey, it is the only system we have and, while it is inherently unfair, when it works it really works, enabling a bestselling book to sell hundreds of thousands, even millions of copies.
- Each stage of the process is intended to ensure that the customers of each bookshop have a range of books on display that are appropriate to their tastes and demographic. Your local indie selects books they think you will enjoy and want to read, and the big chains attempt to do likewise.
- A big retail promotion, such as the 3 for 2 that Waterstones ran for many years, can sell loads of books, tens of thousands, in a short space of time.
- For publishers, it can be nice to leave the actual selling of books to someone else.

CONS

- You can clearly see that this is massively weighted in favour of the big publishers who get more access to retailers, have bigger budgets to spend on fancy presentations and marketing contributions and tend to have long-term ongoing relationships with retailers.
- It is hard for a small publisher, producing one book a month, to get that book in front of key retailers – and thus to get it into the hands of readers via bookshops.
- The weaknesses of this model have been cleverly exploited by Amazon, which can appear to stock every book that comes out. This makes Amazon bigger and more powerful, while also making it harder for independent bookshops to compete.
- There is a dilution of revenue for all parties, with each taking a cut of the RRP.
- The high discounts required by some retailers can significantly reduce author royalties.

The wholesale model

Just a short aside on wholesalers before we end this chapter. Many smaller bookshops don't actually buy their books direct from publishers and instead buy them from wholesalers. These are companies who take all the information coming from publishers, collate it, and present and sell the books to a range of independent bookshops and other retailers that sell books, such as garden centres and gift shops.

PROS

- Publishers rely on wholesalers to deal with hundreds and thousands of smaller retail accounts which saves them the bother of doing so, keeping costs down.
- Wholesalers are generally one-stop book suppliers, able to deliver most books to shops within a day or two. So it can be easier for retailers to manage and stay on top of orders with one or two suppliers than hundreds of separate publishers.

CONS

- The discounts offered to shops are lower than those the big retailers get direct from publishers, as the wholesaler needs to take their cut.

3

The Mathematics of Publishing

When you think about the world of writing and publishing you probably picture an industry built upon words. And rightly so. The book world would be nothing without the written word. But numbers play a crucial part too, and some of the numbers that crunch away behind the scenes of publishing may surprise you.

This section will look at those numbers in some detail – sales figures, costs, percentages – but it is a very long time since I took my maths 'O' level so I will keep things relatively simple. I will also let you in on a few trade secrets; just don't tell anyone you heard them from me.

Sales

How many copies does a book need to sell to become a bestseller?

100,000? 50,000? 10,000?

Each week the *Sunday Times* in the UK publishes four separate book charts – top tens in Hardback Fiction, Hardback General (which is essentially where all the non-fiction goes), Paperback Fiction and Paperback General. In the US, the *New York Times* does a similar thing. Both newspapers pay to have the rights to publish their country's official book sales data and have been doing so for decades, so they are seen as the charts that matter. For a book to be able to feature the three magic words '*Sunday Times* Bestseller', or four magic words '*New York Times* Bestseller' on the cover, it needs to have appeared in one of these charts for at least one week.

But how hard is that to do?

In the UK, to sit at the top of these charts, especially Paperback Fiction, you generally need to sell many thousands of copies. But pick a quiet time of year, perhaps February or March, and you could sneak in at number 10 in the Hardback Non-Fiction chart by selling around 500 copies, a somewhat less daunting figure. Hardbacks sell fewer copies than paperbacks, you see, as they are more expensive, unwieldy, rubbish for reading on the commute and more painful if you drop them on your toes.

Let's put those sales in perspective. There are close to

5,000 book outlets in the UK. A book could sell one copy in just 10% of these locations in any given week and hit the bestseller chart. 90% of shops wouldn't need to have sold any at all, and you'd still have a bestseller on your hands. Seriously, if any hardback book sold just one copy in every branch of WH Smith, for example, it would almost certainly be in the *Sunday Times* top ten.

Things are very different at the top of the charts, of course. The bestselling paperback novel in the UK would typically have to sell well into five figures, although that could be anywhere between 10,000 and 90,000 depending on the time of year and what books are out that week.

It all gets more interesting when you start to delve into the chart data a bit more. The *Sunday Times* top tens are taken from a much larger sales report generated by Nielsen Bookscan. They create a Top 5,000 chart each week that is distributed widely within the book trade, with retailers and publishers poring over the figures to see where they might be missing sales or to stare jealously at someone else's success.

Let's say the bestselling book in the country sold 25,000 copies in a week. That's a lot of books, but not many titles can deliver that level of sales. In the same week it is likely that the tenth bestselling book sold around 7,000 copies – still a lot, but quite a drop off. The book at number 100 in the charts will have sold 1,500 or so. The book at 500 may actually have sold 500 copies, and you can often get into the bottom regions of the Top 5,000 by selling 50 or so copies in a week.

But hang on, Scott. Earlier you told us that we could have a bestseller if we sold just 500 copies. Now you are saying that a book would be No 500 in the charts if it sold that amount, that's hardly a bestseller. Well done readers, I am glad you have been paying attention, but don't forget, the charts you see in the newspapers are collated and grouped by genre. So the tenth bestselling hardback non-fiction title is often only the 500th-bestselling book in the land, when you factor in all books in all formats and genres. Likewise, you could have the eleventh bestselling paperback fiction title and not appear on the *Sunday Times* chart at all, but be selling thousands a week more than the book that is at number ten in that pesky hardback non-fiction chart. The lesson here is to write non-fiction if you want an easier route to the bestseller charts.

How do these sales pan out across an entire year? In a very good year, the bestselling book in the UK can sell close to a million copies, sometimes more, but it would more often be about half that number. The tenth bestseller may have sold half that again. The book at 500 might have sold around 50,000, and you could have the 5,000th-bestselling book of the year by selling 5,000 copies – or just one copy in every bookshop in the land during the year.

America, as many of its inhabitants like to remind everyone on a regular basis, is a much bigger country so book sales are generally higher, but not proportionally so. A bestseller in the US might sell 50-100% more than in the UK but, of course, the two markets vary greatly in terms of what sells and which authors are popular. No matter, the basic principles apply: there is a big drop off after the top few sellers and there is a very long tail of titles that tick over, year in year out.

Costs

How much does it cost to publish a book?

The sales figures we have just examined are all well and good, and may prove fascinating, but you cannot sell a single book until it is printed and distributed to shops, and that can be a costly exercise.

Different types of books have different budgets – a big, illustrated, coffee-table book will usually cost several times more to produce than a fairly straightforward paperback – but for this example we are going to look at the costs for a standard novel with no fancy design elements or illustrations. We are also going to assume that every stage of the process that can be farmed out to a third-party has been, so that all the possible costs for a book are captured.

In 'The Life-cycle of a Book' chapter we looked at the various stages that go into creating a book and these all cost money, but let's break that down. Obviously different editors and designers charge different fees, and editorial costs are often based on word-count, but typical costs at the time of going to press look a bit like this:

Developmental edit: **£1,250**
Copyedit: **£600**
Typesetting: **£400**
Proofread: **£250**

So that is **£2,500** just to get the text ready. A cover design could range from £400 to £800 for a professional designer to produce and lay out an entire cover, so let's go in the middle:

Cover design: **£600**

As we have seen earlier, the cost of printing a book depends on the number you are printing. We will assume a fairly average print run of 3,000 copies at 75p per copy:

Printing: **£2,250**

This brings our grand total for editing, designing and printing the book to **£5,350**. On top of this, the publisher will need to pay warehouse and distribution fees (usually a percentage of sales revenue) and marketing and publicity costs (which could be zero, of course, or could be many thousands of pounds). So I would say that **£6,000** is a reasonable estimate of the cost, to a publisher, of producing a book. And that is before a single copy has been sold.

It is, of course, entirely possible to produce a book for less, and it will often cost a hell of a lot more, but I am looking at typical costs for a traditional publisher using reputable professionals to complete each stage of the process. So let's take that figure of £6,000 into our next section and explore the sort of revenue a publisher can generate from a book.

Revenue

How much money does a publisher make from a book?

So, a publisher has spent £6,000 to produce, sell, distribute and promote 3,000 copies of a new novel. Let's assume all 3,000 copies sell to bookshops, a rare feat but one that makes our maths a little easier, and that it has a recommended retail price of £7.99.

Publishers give book retailers a discount from the RRP which can be anywhere from 30% to 70% depending on the size of the retailer, how many copies they are ordering and whether or not the book goes into a big promotion, but let's use 55% as an average. That means that for every copy sold to bookshops the publisher receives £3.59. Across 3,000 copies that comes to £10,770 of revenue.

We already know that it cost £6,000 to produce and print the book, so by selling 3,000 copies the publisher has made a profit of £4,770. Not too bad.

Oh wait! We forgot returns. In the UK, most books are sold to retailers on a sale-or-return basis. This means that shops can return unsold stock and typically around 20% of all books sold to retailers are sent back. So that £10,770 mentioned above may end up being more like £8,600 once the returns are accounted for. This leaves profit at £2,600.

And the author gets a royalty for every copy of the book sold (less returns), typically 7.5% of the RRP for a paperback. Now, that is very nice for you as the author, and you have earned it, but it is another £1,400 that will need to come out as far as the publisher is concerned, reducing the profit to £1,200.

But a profit is still a profit, right? Well, when you bear in mind that our example assumes that all 3,000 copies sell initially and contains minimal marketing or publicity costs, and fairly average costs for all other elements, you can see why most books struggle to break even. And this is just an analysis of costs specific to one individual book. We haven't remotely considered the broader costs of running a publishing house, big or small, such as rent, rates, employment expenses, equipment and so on.

So how do publishers make any money from their books? Well, the truth is that many do not. They are often reliant on one or two books selling in excess of 10,000 copies, and ideally *lots* more than that, in order to generate the income needed to fund the other books on the list that sell below 3,000. Given time, they can build up a backlist of older titles that tick over, generating ongoing revenue. And ebooks can help too; they are cheaper to sell, as there are no warehouse costs and no returns, and many a book these days moves into profit, eventually, on the back of healthy digital sales. But the overall picture is pretty consistent across publishing: most books struggle to break even.

Royalties

And how much money can an author make?

We have already looked at how the various publishing models work so you should know the score when it comes to royalties: for every copy of a book that sells the author receives a percentage of the revenue. There are many variations on the basic deal but, if we continue with our example of a paperback novel, typically an author will receive 7.5% of the RRP for each copy that sells. On our £7.99 paperback that would be just *under* 60p, but I am feeling generous so will round it up.

Again, sticking with our example, if we sell 3,000 copies, and get 20% of them returned, then the author will have made £1,400 in royalties. Hardly a life-changing amount, but enough to keep you in cookies for a long time to come.

But let's not focus on such tiny numbers. Instead, let's be ambitious and bold and go back to the bestsellers that we discussed earlier. Remember that bestselling book that sold 25,000 copies in a week, taking it to the top of the charts? Assuming it was a £7.99 paperback, that book will have earned its author £15,000 in just one week. The book at No 10, selling 7,000, will have generated £4,200. And even the No 500 book will have made £300, which isn't bad for one week's work.

Although don't forget that the agent will take 15% of that!

And then we need to think about high discount clauses. Most traditional book contracts have a special clause that allows the publisher to pay a lower royalty if they sell a book to a retailer at a 'high discount'. The thing is, these so-called high discounts kick in at 50% and, in reality, nearly all sales to big retailers are at 50% discount or more, and any books in a big promotion are often supplied at 60% discount or even higher. What this means for most authors is that the majority of their book sales deliver a lower royalty. Typically discounts between 50% and 59% will deliver a 6% royalty and discounts of 60%+ will deliver a royalty of 4%. We can safely assume that the bulk of sales of the books in the bestseller charts are at high discount and low royalty.

You may well have seen articles in recent years that look at how hard it is for authors to make a living from writing, and they are broadly accurate. Even authors who are lucky enough to have an ongoing readership for their work need to write a book every year or two to keep the income coming in. It is only a handful of authors at the very top of the bestseller charts who receive six- or seven-figure advances. Most of us will, if we are lucky, make a few thousand pounds a year and not be able to give up the day job.

The end result

What does this all add up to?

It is important that authors understand the numbers behind the publishing world. If a book becomes a bestseller then it is possible for both author and publisher to make a lot of money, and even a moderate seller can, over a long period, generate some decent income. However, the majority of books published will only make a small amount of money for their authors. For most of us, this is not a 'get rich quick' industry. Does that matter? Only you can answer that, but if you have decided to write a book in order to make your fortune, you are probably going to be disappointed. If, however, you are writing a book because you want to share your story, and you value a connection with readers above all else, then great fortune can await – it just may not be a financial one.

Writing
Your
Book

Although I feel as if all I have been doing recently is writing this book, I do actually spend most of my time, and make most of my living, editing other people's books, both for publishers and private clients. My job as an editor is to help the author to make the book as good as it can be, to guide them with friendly prompts, constructive suggestions and, sometimes, forceful persuasion. Often what I am doing is pre-empting issues that readers would have if they were reading the same version I am and trying to ensure the author addresses these, but at the same time I want the book to remain as close to the author's vision as possible. It is part instruction, part observation, and part negotiation.

Every manuscript I work on is, of course, unique but over the years I have come to recognise certain patterns, certain habits, and certain themes that crop up time and time again. In this section of my book I want to share these with you and help you avoid them in your own writing.

However, this is not intended as a comprehensive guide on how to write a book, rather it is a collection of tips and strategies. I will cover what I consider to be the most important aspects of writing fiction but if you want an in-depth tutorial on, say, writing dialogue or creating realistic characters, then there are whole books, online courses, and tutorials dedicated to these subjects and you can spend weeks and months delving into them to improve your work. What I am trying to do is capture the most common mistakes and areas for improvement and explain how to avoid or address them so that, hopefully, you can fix them yourselves.

You may choose to study each of the subjects covered in this section in depth, or you might just want to dip into the areas you feel are relevant to you. I would advise, though, that you at least flick through and make sure that you are not guilty of any of these common errors before you decide your book is ready for the next step.

4

Writing Strategies

Before we get stuck into the nuts and bolts of writing, let's just pause and consider the *act* of writing for a moment. The process. Every writer is different, every book is different, but at some point we all have to sit down and write the bloody thing. Here are some strategies and suggestions that might help get you into the zone.

Just get on with it

If you insist on waiting till conditions are perfect for writing then you'll probably never type a word. It is great if you can find the right desk, the ideal time of day, clear all other jobs, turn off your phone, create the right mood or whatever, but the truth is you'll need to find a way to write *despite* lots of other things getting in the way. At some point you just need to start writing so try not to put that off for too long.

Little and often

I once had breakfast with the novelist David Mitchell. This was many years ago, before *Cloud Atlas* had become a global hit. He and I are a similar age and I think we both had young kids at the time. He asked me if I wrote at all and I told him that I used to but had got out of the habit, what with a full-time job and parenting, etc. What he said next has stayed with me ever since:

> *Just write a little bit every day. Even a line or a paragraph. It all adds up in the end.*

Or something like that. I was busy scoffing bacon and eggs at the time so I may not remember it word for word. The gist has stayed with me, though. If real life keeps you busy, you can always make time to write something, even if it is just a little something. And then, over an extended period, those little somethings grow into something bigger.

Stick to a routine

This method definitely isn't for everyone but it is something that a lot of writers swear by, so it is worth considering even if your initial response is negative. Creating a writing routine, and one that you are disciplined about and follow as closely as possible, can yield great results.

You might be like Haruki Murakami, who gets up at 4am and writes for five or six hours before going for a run in the afternoon, relaxing in the evening and tucking himself up in bed by 9pm. He does this every day when he is writing and he finds the repetition is the key to producing good work.

Of course, few people have the luxury of being able to do that. You could well have a full-time job which only gives you a small window of time in which to write, but by committing to using that window to write on a regular basis you are creating your own routine. You might get up early and write for an hour before your commute, or write on the train in to work, or after dinner on weekdays, or in long shifts at weekends. Whatever works for you, it is the structure that can really help. You know when you'll be writing and how you'll fit it into your day, you get used to the system and you could well find yourself automatically slipping into writing mode when your routine kicks in.

Set a word-count

Many writers like to set themselves the target of writing a certain amount of words each day, or each week. This can certainly boost your sense of achievement and help you make tangible progress towards completing your book. I worry slightly that it can lead to disappointment if you don't hit your target but on balance it does seem like a good way to just, well, keep at it and get nearer to your goal.

Use a spreadsheet

My friend Sarah Franklin is now a successful novelist and university lecturer, but when she was writing her first book she was juggling freelance work with some teaching and also raising two young kids. Her approach to writing was to create a list of tasks, whether they be writing certain scenes, or doing some research, or working on the plot, and allocate an amount of time to each. She would enter them on a spreadsheet, colour coded according to type of job – writing, research, revising – and ranked based on time. She would then plan her week with this in mind. If she knew she'd be spending 60 minutes sitting in a car park while her boys had a swimming lesson then she'd find a piece of work she could complete in that time. It is a great system if you know you'll only have short periods in which you can work, or if you are trying to manage lots of other jobs alongside your writing.

Create a writing plan

Even if you don't want to go into full spreadsheet mode, it does make sense to have a plan in place. Research suggests that we get more work completed when we create a To Do list, or some similar written plan. You can plan the book itself and you can plan the writing of it. Introducing structure to your writing can reap dividends.

Take a break

Sometimes 30 minutes away from the computer screen or writing pad can be as useful as two hours in front of them. Give yourself permission to do something else. Once you have done a decent stint of writing, go for a walk, bake a cake, watch an episode of a TV show, play some music and dance around the house, have a nap. Do something that isn't writing. Give your brain and creativity a rest and you will more often than not come back to your book energised and ready for another burst of genius. You may even have solved that plot problem without realising it.

You don't have to start at the beginning

It isn't compulsory to sit down and start writing your book with Chapter One. You may have a complete idea of the final scene of your book but are not yet sure how to get there. Well, write that final scene first. Write any content that excites you, that you are eager to get down on paper. You can write the entire book out of sequence if that works for you, and then piece it together at the end. When you are getting started it is the writing that matters, not the order in which you do it.

Avoid distractions

I write and edit for a living so most days I am sitting at a computer screen with the need to work, uninterrupted, for a period of time. None of my electronic devices have notifications switched on. If I receive a text, tweet, email or any other communication I don't know anything about it until I look for it. Now, I realise the mere idea of this puts The Fear into many people but I find it allows me to do the job I am supposed to be doing without too many distractions. To be fair, that doesn't stop the postman knocking at the door with a delivery, but it does block out the majority of beeps, pings and pop-ups that can divert my attention away from writing. Try doing the same while *you* are writing. I have actually carried the discipline on into my non-writing time too: I never receive notifications, and I am convinced my life is better as a result. Deal with that sort of stuff when you want to, not when it first appears. Having said all that, I nearly always have music playing while I write and I don't find that a distraction at all.

Shit happens

Most of us are not able to write full-time. We have to pay the bills, raise a family, walk the dog, cook dinner or any number of chores, and these real-life things can sometimes get in the way of our writing progress. Or some days you are just not in the mood. It happens. Don't beat yourself up over it. You need to give yourself permission to *not* write occasionally.

Find out what works

You probably won't get it right first time so feel free to adjust your writing strategy as you learn more about what works and what doesn't. You might start out by getting up early and trying to write for a few hours in the morning but discover that you are not very productive at that time and, actually, a concerted effort after lunch or in the evening delivers the best results. You may be great at writing for long periods, several hours at a time, or you may write better in fits and starts. If you are new to this, and if this is your first book, you probably don't know the best way to write it just yet. Don't be afraid of trying different things.

You can leave stuff out

If you are unsure how to tackle a scene, or quite what to write at a particular point, then just put in a note or a piece of holding text [Scott, remember to write a bit more here later] and you can come back to it another time, perhaps leaving it till your next draft. Don't wade through a section of your book that isn't working for you – flag it and move on.

Remember, you are already a writer

If you are finding the idea of writing 1,000+ words a day a little bit daunting then perhaps just remind yourself that you already write loads of stuff every single day, whether that be emails, text, tweets, Facebook posts, or memos and reports at work. Most of us write hundreds, if not thousands of words, on a daily basis without really giving it too much thought.

The difference with writing a book is that you *are* giving it thought, a lot of thought, but step back a second and you may realise that the physical act of writing is something you have already mastered. You can do this.

These are just some ideas and suggestions to consider. You may need to try a few of them, or combine some, before you find a system that works for you. It may be that you end up trying something completely different or creating your own strategy. How you do it is far less important than actually doing it. This book won't write itself, so find a way to get it written.

5

Dialogue

Let's start with a simple truth that may surprise you.

Writing realistic dialogue is a waste of time.

There you go. I've said it now and can't take it back. While I will, on these pages, advocate the need for authentic characters, believable plots and realistic world-building, I will not be urging you to be quite so honest and truthful with the words that come out of your characters' mouths. And here's why.

In real life, the conversations most of us have, the majority of the time, are really fucking boring. They are full of redundancies, non sequiturs, pauses, umms and ahhs and content that only really makes sense to the sender and recipient. Don't believe me? Try jotting down, word for word, the next conversation you overhear. It could read something like this, or a variation thereon.

'So, yeah, well, no, and then I told them that, um, you know, er, that I didn't want to… What was that noise?… Anyway, yeah, told them that, didn't I?'

'No way.'

'I did, right. And then, well, er, then they didn't even bother to reply.'

'That's terrible. Same thing happened to my brother.'

'Wuh? Which one?'

'Davey. Youngest. You know, you met him that time, yeah, that time when we were at that thing, the thing for Maria's birthday.'

I will stop there, even though I am sure you are totally gripped. I do not present this as an example of poor dialogue, or a complaint about how kids today speak to one another, or any other social commentary. The thing is, if you noted the content of any conversation between two people, whether it be gossiping with friends, a discussion of the latest political situation, or an in-depth debate about rocket science, more often than not you'd find it full of stuff that just looks awful written down. It might be more 'honest' to show your characters speaking in this way but it would be a massive pain in the arse to read.

Also, much of everyday conversation is about fairly dull topics – the weather, what is for dinner, what you are up to later, why you haven't fixed that squeaky door hinge yet. And that is fine, because these conversations are happening in real life and are not taking up lines on a page or attempting to explain our characters or progress the 'plot' of our lives. They are just words we throw out there, usually without thinking. Also, I'll fix the hinge once I have finished writing this book so you can stop going on about it now.

When we pick up a novel we are, whether we are aware of it or not, entering into a silent contract with the author. We know, and they know, that the contents within are not 'real' but we are willing to suspend our disbelief and go with the story they tell us because we want to be entertained, or informed, or moved. And if there are startling inaccuracies in the story – it is set in the 19th century but someone is wearing a digital watch, or a character acts in an inauthentic way just because the plot needs them to – then we feel let down. But we are more than happy to let the author present us with dialogue that is cleaned and tidied up for the page. This usually takes three forms:

First, the author doesn't bother us with the bits of dialogue that don't progress plot or character. We don't see much 'Hello', 'How are you?' or 'What time is it?' in novels.

Second, we accept that the dialogue we do see has the boring and awkward bits removed, in most cases. No 'umms' or 'ahhs' or the modern habit of 'Yeah, no' before every reply.

And third, most dialogue in fiction ignores the fact that in real conversations people talk over each other, overlap and mishear. Real conversations are often a bit of a jumble. Garbled dialogue on the page is not a great look.

So there you have it, permission to present the reader with dialogue that isn't strictly realistic. But don't think that lets you off the hook; there are still loads of things you need to consider and mistakes you need to avoid. I will throw these at you on the following few pages. Brace yourself.

To " or not to "

There are a few different ways to present dialogue within a text and which one you use is completely up to you but do be aware that some readers get all fidgety when authors don't conform to what they perceive as the norm.

The norm, of course, is the use of quotation marks. Let's start with double quotation marks, or speech marks.

"Thanks for reading my book," said Scott.

This tends to be the method we were all taught at school and is the one most people are comfortable with. If you fall into that camp then that is absolutely fine for your manuscript but do please try to remember the rules. Punctuation remains within the speech marks, so not:

"Thanks for reading my book", said Scott.

Which is something I see far more than I would like.

The dialogue tag, as we call it, that follows the speech is part of the same sentence so should not look like this:

"Thanks for reading my book." Said Scott.

Which is an even more common error.

If you want to put a tag or gesture or other break in the middle of some speech then punctuate accordingly, again treating the whole thing as one sentence.

> *"Thanks," said Scott with a charming smile, "for reading my book."*

As a very rough rule of thumb when punctuating speech, check to see if the sentence would still make sense if you took the speech marks away. If it would, then the chances are you are OK.

Having said all that, readers in the UK will find that novels on their bookshelves tend to use single quotation marks.

> *'Thanks for reading my book,' said Scott.*

This is just one of those weird UK/US style differences. In the same way as Americans like to remove the letter U from perfectly reasonable words such as 'flavour' and 'colour',[8] Brits like to remove one of the ' from ". The reason, as I understand it, is that on this side of the pond we feel that too many little apostrophe-like symbols hanging around at the top of a line is unsightly, a bit busy, so we clean things up a bit by cutting them in half.

Don't worry, though. You should use whichever style works for you. It will not harm your chances of being published. Each publisher has a house style and they'll pay a copyeditor to make sure all of this stuff is correct, so even if they prefer a different way of doing it to your way, it can all be sorted later.

You may, if you wish, want to discard quotation marks

---

8   Don't get me started on their inexplicable addition of the letter S to Lego.

completely. It drives some readers up the wall but, hey, they need to lighten up a bit.

—Thanks for reading my book, said Scott.
—You're welcome, the reader replied.

Apologies if the above lines gives you the heebie-jeebies but it is a style of presenting speech that has become more common in contemporary fiction. Personally, I like it because it reduces the amount of punctuation and, for me, improves the flow of my reading. Some authors like to go one stage further and remove all indication of speech – the radicals.

Thanks for reading my book, said Scott.

For some readers, of course, this is a step too far and they find themselves getting lost in the text and unsure which bits are speech and which are narrative. You do need to be aware of that, and if you are writing what you consider to be a commercial novel then an experimental style of presenting dialogue would be a risky option. An avant-garde work of literary fiction, on the other hand, and anything goes.

My advice is to use the style that feels natural for you but please, on behalf of editors everywhere, be consistent.

Make each character sound different

Although we kicked off this chapter with an explanation of why dialogue in fiction is never truly realistic, there is still a lot you can do to make it feel authentic. One way is to ensure that every one of your characters speaks in a slightly different way. This can be a pig to get right but the pay-off is huge and it is worth the effort.

You don't have to create a unique and bespoke speaking pattern for every character, although feel free if the mood takes you, but it makes sense to give some thought to how each person would speak. Things to bear in mind include: Does this character tend to be long-winded? Do they swear a lot? Are they direct and to the point? Are they often sarcastic? Are they softly spoken or forceful? How do you imagine this character speaking and can you do your best to convey that on the page?

You may also want to consider where they come from, what job they do, what sort of person they speak to most often. A character who spends much of the day at home with their children may well speak differently in general conversation, or have different topics of conversation, than someone who works in a call centre and spends all day speaking to strangers, or a teacher who stands at the front of the classroom for hours on end.

A good way to test how well you are doing is to look

at a piece of dialogue that extends beyond a sentence or two and see if it is obvious who is speaking just from *how* they are speaking and what they are saying. It won't always be possible but if you are able to achieve this with some regularity then your manuscript should be in a good place.

The important thing is to ensure that your characters don't all sound the same when they are speaking. You need to mix it up a bit, otherwise the characters are just cardboard cut-outs mouthing words you have given them to say.

To whom are they speaking?

Take a look at each piece of dialogue and ask yourself who is speaking to whom. We all moderate our speech depending on the person we are speaking to and your characters should do the same. I do not speak to my mother the same way I speak to my daughter. I don't speak to someone I have just met in the same way as an old friend. Figures of authority are often spoken to more formally or politely than shopkeepers. Just a simple sense check – are these people speaking to each other in a way that feels authentic for the situation? – can really improve the quality of your dialogue.

Some things are better left unsaid

Here are two versions of a similar exchange:

> *'You OK?'*
> *'Fine.'*

and

> *'You OK?'*
> *'Actually I am feeling really down today. My boss is being annoying and the boiler broke last week and isn't fixed yet so I can't have a hot shower and I was supposed to be going to this thing tonight and I am not sure I can be bothered.'*

One contains loads more information than the other, but the first example is, I would argue, far more realistic and more likely to happen in real life. Your readers are clever people, they can read between the lines. They are used to having a conversation where the 'truth' is not actually spoken out loud. They are also used to reading cues from the person speaking. Try this for size:

> *'You OK?'*
> *Laura stared off into the distance for a moment, as*

if distracted by something going on behind me, before emitting a brief sigh. 'Fine,' she said.

I am not suggesting the above is exemplary prose but I would say that it conveys much more than the three words of dialogue that are actually spoken. I am not filling the gaps, but I am hinting that there are gaps to be filled, and that can be far more interesting to read than two characters who explain everything to each other.

Do not be afraid to leave things unspoken.

Avoid exposition and info dumps

If you attend one of my workshops or classes then you'd have a reasonable expectation that I would impart lots of advice and information in the things I say. After all, you'd have paid good money for that very thing. However, the vast majority of day-to-day dialogue is not a detailed exchange of information, so when dialogue in a novel does try to convey lots of info it can come across as clunky.

Exposition is where a chunk of background information, backstory or an explanation of some kind is presented to the reader. Sometimes you really need the reader to know a particular fact for the plot to make sense, but conveying that through dialogue needs some skill and dexterity.

> *'Nice place you have here, thanks for inviting me.'*
> *'You are more than welcome. The house was built in 1854 and was owned by the same family for more than 150 years before we bought it. The previous owner left in mysterious circumstances, apparently.'*

The above displays almost no skill or dexterity. I don't believe someone would say this stuff in such a direct way and it is bloody obvious that the 'mysterious circumstances' will come back and have an important part to play in the plot. That's what I mean by clunky. We can all see what is going on here and it lacks subtlety. You could get the same information across within dialogue by extending the conversation, having the visitor ask a few questions, letting the chat warm up gradually and revealing little bits of information as it progresses, interspersed with other bits and pieces so that it is not so clunky and artificial.

Info dumps, big chunks of information delivered through speech, are a similar issue and best avoided. They are incredibly dull to read.

One phrase that always rings alarm bells ringing for me is 'As you know', as it is nearly always followed by a load of information that the author is shoehorning into the conversation.

> *'As you know, this car is capable of speeds in excess of 180mph and was voted best sports car in its class last year.'*

If the other character knows this, why tell them? The only answer is 'because the author needs the reader to know it'.

Mix it up

The bulk of most conversations comprises small, brief exchanges that go back and forth and progress and lubricate the dialogue. It is fine to present a conversation entirely made up of short pieces of speech but beware of letting things go on for too long as it can become a bit too much like watching a tennis match or reading a play.

Conversely, it is rare for someone to utter a paragraph-length piece of speech which then receives a paragraph in return and so on. Two or three pages of big, detailed speeches can be a real slog to get through and I can't think of too many examples of where this would be worth doing.

Ideally, across the length of your novel, you would vary things somewhat. Don't present us with the same sort of dialogue every time. Some short exchanges – great. Lengthy speeches where they make sense within the context of the story – lovely. Conversations that are a mixture of short and long speech – perfect. Variation is key.

Think about pace

If you are writing a thriller and we are in the final few pages, with anticipation building for the climax, you probably don't want to present the reader with big chunks of lengthy dialogue, as they will slow things down. You want things to be pacey, and shorter exchanges can help achieve that.

Consider where the dialogue is coming in your book and how you want people to read it. Slow and languid will be fine at certain points, fast and furious better at others.

He said, she said

Now for an important public service announcement regarding dialogue tags.

Dialogue tags are the words before or after speech that tell the reader who was speaking.

'So now you know what a dialogue tag is,' said Scott.

They are some of the nuts and bolts that hold your book together but there are certain things that are worth bearing in mind when using them.

Although they might not be aware they are doing it, readers tend to ignore the word 'said' when it appears in a text. Perhaps ignore is not quite the right word; they absorb it. Just as a comma tells them to pause, but in their head they are not saying the word 'comma', 'said' gives them a bit of information about who has spoken but they tend to gloss over it. It moves things along; they are so used to seeing it, and are aware of what it signifies, that it is treated as less important and there is no need to linger on it. If you use the word 'said', do not expect people to notice it.

The same is not the case when you choose a less standard

word – replied, interjected, shouted, ejaculated, screamed, opined – so when you use such a word it will stand out, the reader will notice and will not gloss over it. Ask yourself this question before using an alternative to 'said': Do I want the reader to pause and notice the word I am using? Occasionally the answer will be a big fat YES. More often than not you just want them to go with the flow of the dialogue and then, no matter how much you want your character to ejaculate, you would do better to hold them off.

And this is doubly, triply, quadruply so when it comes to using adverbs, Scott said seriously. Plonking an adverb in a dialogue tag really makes it stand out and the situations when that is a good idea are very few and far between. Often an adverb is redundant anyway:

'Just piss off and leave me alone,' Scott said angrily.

I think the words I am saying speak for themselves here. If you need the addition of 'angrily', or any adverb to make your point, then I would suggest your dialogue isn't really working hard enough for you.

Varied and adverb-heavy dialogue tags are, I think, the most common thing I have to remove when I am editing a manuscript. I know why they proliferate – the author thinks 'said' is boring and repetitive and wants their prose to read in a more literary manner – but they are not needed anywhere near as much as they appear.

And finally on dialogue tags, do you really need them at all? If there are only two people taking part in a conversation then, after you have established who is saying what initially, we can work the rest out for ourselves. The convention is that the speakers take it in turns, so you can tell us that Deirdre has said something and then that Bob has said something in reply but after that we'll assume the conversation goes Deirdre/Bob/Deidre/Bob until you tell us otherwise.

Use of character names

'In real life we don't use people's names in conversation anywhere near as often as characters seem to do in unedited manuscripts.'

'Is that right, Scott?'

'Yes it is, Reader.'

'I must say that I hadn't noticed that but now you mention it, Scott, I realise I do it all the time.'

'And now you have noticed, Reader, it looks a bit odd, doesn't it?'

'Yes it does, Scott. Thanks so much for pointing it out.'

'Reader, it is not even remotely a problem. Consider it a reward for purchasing my book.'

New paragraphs

This is a small thing but I see writers get it wrong a lot. You should start every new piece of dialogue by opening speech marks but you do not close them until that person has finished speaking. You do, however, have to open speech marks for every new paragraph within a speech.

> *'Here I am chatting away quite happily in paragraph one but for the purposes of this illustration I shall end it shortly. Please note that I will not use closing speech marks.*
>
> *'Instead I move to a new paragraph and use opening speech marks again. How exciting.*
>
> *'And I do the same thing again here, although this time I will end the speech and close things off like so.'*

The above indicates that it was all one speech. If I were to close the speech marks at the end of each paragraph the reader would assume someone else was speaking the next one.

Speech within speech

Sometimes a character will quote someone else's words or speech. If you are using standard speech punctuation, this is how you show it on the page.

> *'And so she said to me, "Scott, I really love your chapter on dialogue," and I told her how good it was to hear that.'*

You see how the quoted speech uses double inverted commas but the main speech uses single? You just flip that round if you are using double inverted commas for the speech in your book and use single for the quoted speech.

Press 'record'

You can learn a lot about how dialogue works by recording some. Don't be a weirdo and place bugs around the house, or sneakily record people at your local coffee shop, but ask friends or family if you can record a chat and then pop your smartphone on the table and try to forget about it. After a few minutes the conversation should fall back into a fairly normal style. Later, try transcribing it and see what you discover. You will notice patterns and rhythms, the way people use each other's names, how they often leave things unspoken, and potentially lots of other details that will a) inform the way you write dialogue and b) show you what you are currently doing wrong. The idea is not to replicate what they say word for word, but to learn more about how conversations flow.

Don't use 'do not'

In modern speech we use contractions – don't, won't, shan't, would've – far more than the full version. You will hear 'I don't like that' far more often than 'I do not like that' so your dialogue should reflect that. The full version still has its place, especially when someone is angry or trying to make a point, but use it sparingly.

We didn't always speak this way

People don't speak the same way now as they did in the 1970s, or the 1930s, or the 1820s, or – you get the idea – so give some thought to the historical setting of your book. There tends to be a bit of negotiation needed in order for your dialogue to make sense to a contemporary reader – you certainly don't want your medieval character to say 'OK' or 'don't kill my vibe' but you may not need to go completely 'thee', 'thou' and 'forsooth' either.

Research the period, read books written at the time, use online dictionaries or Google Ngram[9] to see when a particular word or phrase was first coined, and generally ensure that what your characters say makes sense for the time without getting in the way of understanding for the modern reader.

Vocative commas

If you know what a vocative comma is then you don't need to read this bit. If the term is new to you then please continue, reader.

Although I have said that you don't need your characters

---

9   More on this in the Resources section later.

to say each other's names all the bloody time, when they do use them you will need to employ a vocative comma. The rule is quite simple: when one character addresses another by name, the name is offset by a comma.

'I understand now, Scott.'

Or, perhaps:

'Scott, thanks for explaining that to me.'

Or even:

'OK, Scott, I totally get that.'

You're welcome.

There should be plenty here to help you spruce up your dialogue and, perhaps more importantly, ensure you are not making the classic mistakes that editors and agents see all the time. When you finish your first, or next, draft, it is well worth reading back through your work and looking at the words your characters say to see if you are authentic and consistent.

6

Character

It won't surprise you to learn that creating authentic, well-rounded characters in your novel is a pretty good thing to aim for. The more readers can relate to, empathise with, be scared of or excited by the people who populate your book the more your story will resonate for them. And the flip side of that is also true: fill your book with unrealistic, stereotypical, one-dimensional characters and readers will not care what happens to them.

What follows will, I hope, help you ensure your characters feel real but it is important to note that much of the work you will need to do won't actually end up on the page. You, as the author, need to know your characters inside and out, but your readers do not. Ideally, your deep understanding will inform and drive your characters and that will come across to the reader without you having to shout about it.

Description is your friend
...and your enemy

One very simple way to ensure a reader can picture a character is to describe that character to them. However, an over-reliance on that method can quickly come across as repetitive and lazy. If each time a new character appears, their size, hair and eye colour and other attributes are mentioned, it makes for very predictable and dull writing. My advice is to mix things up a bit. What is it about each character that you want the reader to know? If it is important that the reader realises a character is tall, think of ways you can get that across without writing 'Barbara was tall'. Could you convey it through their own perspective, the fact that they can see over the heads of people in a crowd? Or could other characters help you out? If John has to look up when speaking to Barbara then we get the idea of a height difference between them. It brings us to the whole telling and showing balance issue which I cover in a few chapters from now. It is fine to tell us what a character looks like, but telling us what *every* character looks like, and never showing us, creates an imbalance in your narrative.

In Greek mythology, Helen of Troy is considered to be the most beautiful woman in the world. She appears in both of Homer's epic poems, the *Odyssey* and *Iliad*. In neither story are her physical attributes described. Instead, we get to see the reaction of other people to her, and in those reactions we can tell that she is considered a great beauty. It worked for

Homer, his words are still read millennia after they were first written down, and it will work for you.

The same goes, even more so, for the attributes we cannot see. Much better to show us that someone is brave, or nervous, or spiteful, or excitable, than to simply tell us.

In short, use description wisely and sparingly and it can be effective. Use it too much and your narrative risks being bland and your characters risk being one- or two-dimensional.

If you don't know, ask

I am a middle-class, cisgender, able-bodied, straight, white man. I have to recognise that I have benefited from huge privilege in my life without asking for it or needing to do anything to receive it and, more often than not, being unaware of how my position affects others. I do not know what it is like to be a woman, or another ethnicity, what it might have been like to grow up as part of a very rich family, or a very poor one. I can read accounts written by other people and I can do my research but I can't ever really walk in another person's shoes. However, I can ask them.

If you are writing a character that is very different to you in terms of gender, occupation, background or whatever, then make the effort to see if the attitudes and actions you ascribe to them ring true. On a very simple level, if you are a man and your partner is a woman, ask her to read your work to see if you have made any huge and glaring errors with your female characters. You may have friends from different backgrounds, ethnicities, or with different life experiences, whose views may be helpful. Failing that, find books written by people who might have similar experiences to your characters and read what they have to say, or find interviews or articles and read or watch them. You are simply sense-checking the characters you have made. Would a young woman with anxiety issues think and act this way when faced with this situation? You are never going to get everything spot on, but you can make the effort to get pretty close.

Nobody's perfect

We all have flaws. Every one of us. Some of them may be obvious to others, some may be hidden within us. But they *are* present and they need to be present in your characters as well. You may think that writing the 'perfect' man in your rom-com is a good idea, or that creating an invincible heroine for your action adventure will make things more exciting, but they actually reduce the drama, reduce the tension and remove a level of authenticity.

Think about each character's weaknesses. Are they quick to anger? Is it a man who routinely dismisses the opinions of women? Do they have low self-esteem, or are they supremely arrogant? I could spend the next 100 pages listing potential weaknesses but you get the idea. To create a well-rounded, believable character they need to be flawed.

All the great characters in fiction, and history, are – and yours shouldn't be any different.

And no one is all bad

Even the most evil villain will have redeeming features. Perhaps he is kind to his dog, or she is a wonderful mother but absolutely horrible as a boss, maybe they are a patron of the arts, or have a beautiful singing voice, or routinely give money to homeless people sleeping rough. A character that is all bad, with no good at all, lacks depth and becomes a cardboard cut-out.

The story must change them

A central character who is the same at the end of the book as they were at the beginning is not a character most readers will want to spend their time with. Real people change all the time for all sorts of reasons, and fictional characters should too.

One useful tool is to create a character arc for the main players in your story. There are lots of ways of doing this, but you can simply draw a line from left to right and mark on that line the key events that happen to the character in the book. You can also add in, with another colour, any important interactions they have with other characters. Then, in a third colour, mark up how those events and interactions affect them. If you want to get fancy, then make it a wavy line with the ups and downs representing the fate of the character. Do they end up on a high or a low? Does a bad experience early on change them for most of the book? Spending time in advance thinking about how your characters develop as people within the story you plan to tell will help ensure you reflect that as you write.

That is only one technique and there are lots more you can research and try out, but whatever you choose to do I recommend you revisit the character arcs at the end of your main draft. How have your characters changed during the story? If you cannot spot sufficient change, then neither will your readers.

Throw a party

Not literally (although don't let me stop you if you feel like it), but you can have fun by imagining your characters in other situations. If the key characters in your book were all invited to a party, how would they interact with each other? What gift would they bring for the host? Include characters who may not actually meet in the story you are writing. What if they were stuck in a lift? Or involved in a car crash? You don't need to write these scenes out, just imagine them in your head while you are out walking, or wallowing in a bubble bath. You may find you learn more about your characters, or learn where you still have work to do to make them feel real.

Give them a backstory

Many writers find it helpful to create a biography for each character, including a backstory summarising how they got to the point at which we join them in the novel. How much detail you go into is up to you – some authors create quite detailed biographies including all manner of things such as upbringing, school, relationships, jobs, and key events in their past, while others stick to a short pen portrait with headline information only. However you go about it, knowing who your characters are before you start to write them on the page can really help, and a biography is something you can refer back to as the story develops. You can sense-check whether or not a character might make a certain decision or take a particular action based on how they have acted in the past, or you may want to ensure that their perspective on life is consistent with the life they have led. You will probably find that 90% or more of the content of your biographical notes will never feature in the book but they will inform how the character is presented to the reader, and that makes them feel more real.

Send a letter

Here's another piece of advice I stole from David Mitchell. Have your characters write to you. As I understand it,

Mitchell sends himself postcards, letters and emails from his characters when he is trying to visualise them and flesh them out. These communications never make the final book, they are purely a way of making them feel real, but it is an imaginative way to bring fictional characters to life.

What's in a name?

Naming characters can be a lot of fun but it can also prove quite torturous. It definitely needs some thought. And while much of this chapter bangs on about the need for realism and authenticity, there are some aspects of naming characters in novels that need to be artificial.

For example, I know quite a lot of people called Ben. In real life, most of us know more than one person by a particular name. If your novel reflected real life by including some characters with the same first names then it would be bloody confusing for the reader. There are very few novels in which characters share forenames, and when they do it tends to be important to the plot. So, novelists conveniently populate their fictional worlds with people who all happen to have different names.

And that may seem obvious but there is a further consideration to make. Because of the way people read words on a page, taking in groups of words at a time, it can also be confusing if you have characters with similar names, or names that start with the same letter. If your three main characters are called Ben, Bill and Bob, then I can assure you that readers will get them mixed up. Help the reader out by presenting them with clear and different names for the important protagonists in your story.

There is nothing to stop you using the names of real people but if they are famous, or people you know, then you do risk them taking offence at how their namesake is portrayed. The important thing is to find names that work for you, that you can bear to write over and over again, that feel right for the characters you are writing. They are going to stick with you for the rest of your life.

Ethnicity

In some manuscripts that I edit the ethnicity of a character is only mentioned if that character is not white. Whenever I point this out to the authors, who are always white themselves, they are horrified to discover what they have done. There is nothing deliberate or sinister about it but they have projected part of their own perception and worldview onto their story. What this does, of course, is suggest to the reader that white is the norm and any other ethnicity needs to be pointed out.

If the ethnicity of a character is important, and often it won't matter at all, then there are other ways of informing the reader. If you name a character Noburo Watanabe then readers will assume he has some Japanese heritage. Clues can be offered in conversation between characters, or it may come out just from the context of the story. Just ask yourself whether or not it is something you absolutely need to get across and, if you do, find a good way of doing so.

Celebrate difference

Think about your characters' differences. They will, in the main, dress differently, speak differently, have differing views and beliefs. Think about how you can convey that in how they behave in your book.

Internal conflict

Not every character in every novel needs a big noticeable internal conflict but an element of internal conflict is something that can help bring them to life. It could be something huge, such as choosing between love and duty. It might be some sort of repressed desire – an unfulfilled dream to be a ballet dancer. It could be something that seems quite insignificant. Whatever it is, it should inform their personality and how they act, even if just in a small way.

What's their motivation?

We all need things. And sometimes we think we *need* things when actually we just *want* them. But our desire for love, happiness, a new car, a Tunnock's Caramel Wafer, a bit of a dance, revenge, or global domination will be something that informs what we do and how we treat others. Consider the main motivation for your key characters and ensure that what they do in your story is consistent with that.

Relationships

When creating characters and moving them around the page you need to consider how they will act with and react to others. This may be an integral component of your story, such as two characters falling in love, or it may just be adding some texture and colour to a character, such as how they treat their staff. Every interaction a character has will tell the reader something about them, even if only subtly or unconsciously.

A few words about...

In France, back in the days when printing presses and moveable type were used to make books, the cast-iron plate that reproduced the text onto paper was called a *stereotype*. The clicking sound the casting plate made was called a *cliché*. So the words stereotype and cliché come from a repetitive process producing the same thing over and over again.

Nowadays we use the word cliché to refer to an expression that has been used so much it has lost any sense of originality and can be seen as an example of lazy and unimaginative writing. Due to overuse, clichés become tired or stale and lack impact – three things you almost certainly want to avoid with your own writing.

Nerves of steel. It took her breath away. A shiver ran down his spine. Like a hot knife through butter. These are phrases you will be familiar with and you know what they mean without needing to think about it even though none of them are literal. They are instead metaphors and similes, examples of poetry in everyday language, and I don't want to knock any use of poetry. However, as a writer you may want to be careful how you use clichés.

People use clichés regularly in conversation and, if you want your dialogue to reflect real life, then it might be a good idea for your characters to occasionally resort to a cliché when talking, but challenge yourself to avoid them as much as possible in your main narrative. When you come across one, ask yourself if there is a different or more original way of conveying the same concept. Don't feel you can't use any clichés at all but don't rely on them too much.

Clichés are not restricted to words and phrases. You can also have clichéd situations and plot points. The middle-aged professor falling for a younger student. The orphaned child who turns out to be the only person who can save their tribe/nation/planet/universe. A story that opens with a character waking from a dream. These have all been done to death and if you use them you should do so in the knowledge that there is nothing original about them whatsoever.

Which brings us on to stereotypes. Put simply, a stereotype is a clichéd character. A type of person that we have seen countless times before in fiction or in movies. They are predictable in how they look, speak and act, and suck the originality from the book. Some obvious examples are Arab characters as terrorists, a person who spends lots of time on a computer being a geek (we all spend lots of time on computers these days!), the evil step-parent, the high-school jock who treats girls badly and bullies the novel's protagonist. Stereotypes often focus on nationality, ethnicity or gender and you would do well to steer clear of anything obvious or that we've all seen many times before.

...clichés and stereotypes

Keep some secrets

No one else really knows everything there is to know about you. Many of us would get in a lot of trouble if anyone did. And the reader does not need to know everything about your characters. They will work out lots of stuff through context, by what they do, the things they say and how other characters respond to them. But do not feel that you need to share everything. You can keep lots back. Show and tell us enough so that we understand the character and their motivations and then let them do their thing. We do not need to know their DNA sequence in order to enjoy their story.

There are many tricks and techniques you can employ to bring your characters to life, and you may well have to use different ones at different times with different characters, but it is an investment of time and effort that always repays with interest. You want your readers to engage with your character, remain interested in them and, most important of all, you don't want readers to forget them.

7

World-building

World-building is often associated with science fiction and fantasy novels, but it is an important aspect of almost every genre of fiction. Put simply, it is the art of creating a realistic world for your characters, and story, to inhabit. The level and intricacy of the world building you need to do will depend on several things – and clearly a fantasy novel set in a mythical land is going to need more attention in this area than, say, a contemporary novel set in London – but the basic principles are the same.

This chapter will concentrate on those basics – guidelines that could be applied to any narrative. There are whole handbooks dedicated to world-building in science fiction, fantasy and historical fiction and I will gladly point you in their direction for the granular detail of those genres, but right now we will examine the key points and how to implement them within your work whether it is set in the past, present or future, in a suburban street or a thriving metropolis on a distant planet.

Do your research

If your story takes place in a real location then, no matter when it is set, you will be able to research what it looks or looked like, and this should be reflected in your novel. Ideally you would also be able to find out what it sounds like and smells like, how it feels to be there. Visit and spend time in the location if at all possible. Failing that, check out Google Street View, YouTube videos, TV shows or films set there. Once again, you don't need to mention every last detail but if your character would have to pass a bunch of street-food vendors when moving between two locations in real life, they would see, smell and hear all manner of things, and your reader should at least get a whiff of that.

Making history

We have all been somewhere and felt a real sense of the history of the place. Often, I grant you, it is when we are visiting a place that is very old, like a castle or forest or mountain range, but everywhere has some sense of history and it can be shown in many ways.

Spend time in almost any town, city or village and you will be able to spot many decades and often centuries of history all around you. Walk down a London street and you might pass a sleek, modern office block next to a pub that dates back to Tudor times, followed by some Victorian buildings rubbing shoulders with an awful 1980s monstrosity. This is history presenting itself through architecture, a visible sign of the past all around us. We can also see history in road signs and names, in the way towns and cities are laid out – think of how buildings have been repurposed over the years; what was once a bank might now be a restaurant.

But you also need to consider the aspects of history we cannot see. Is your story set in a country that has a class system, or that once had slavery? Are certain types of people more likely to work in certain jobs? What are the major industries? What is the predominant religion? What rules and regulations and laws govern how people act or dress? A book set in Iran would have a very different tone, atmosphere and physical make-up than a book set in New Zealand, because of both their present culture and their very different histories.

Flora and fauna

This may be an obvious point, so I won't dwell on it for too long, but give some thought to the plants and animals that will live in the locations of your novel. Also think about how they may have changed over time. When I was growing up

I would see flocks of sparrows every day and now I cannot remember the last time I saw a single sparrow. What should be growing and living in the time and place your story is set?

Draw a map

You are probably used to seeing maps at the beginning of fantasy novels and many readers find them a useful resource as they navigate their way through deserts and forests and oceans. And while you rarely see a map in a novel set in the present day, that doesn't mean you can't use one when writing it.

A map can serve many functions for the writer but a key one is to ensure you keep everything in the right place. If your narrator lives on a suburban street and commutes to work , they probably take the same route each day. Do they turn left or right out of their house each morning? This may seem like a small detail, and it may not be a detail that needs to make it into the book, but you as the writer need to know it.

That is a very specific and minor point but you can broaden it out in almost any aspect of your fictional world. Who sits where in the office? What mode of transport does your character use to get from A to B, or from B to C, and how long does it take? What scenery will they pass on any particular journey? Or even, what is the layout of the house they live in? A little sketch for key locations, scenes and journeys can help you visualise things more clearly and that, in turn, will make its way into your writing.

What time is it?

Think about the time of day that your scene takes place. What would be happening in that location at that time? A city street at 1pm on a weekday would be busy, with people from offices on their lunch breaks, cycle couriers flying by, perhaps a bit of a traffic jam, horns honking, people trying to get from A to B quickly. The same street at 1am, or at a weekend, would be very different. You can apply identical thinking to a royal palace in a fantasy novel, a space station in a science-fiction novel or a market square in a historical novel. Consider what is likely to be happening in this location at this time of day and reflect it in your scene, even if only in passing.

You can extend this out to cover the time of year, too, or just the weather in general. Clothing changes in summer compared to winter. People are more languid and in less of a rush when it is 30°C outside than when it's a cold, rainy day.

Population control

A common issue I come across in manuscripts is that the author, and therefore the story, is so focused on their main characters that the fictional world they have created can seem devoid of any other people. It is fine to concentrate on the central characters, but do please give the reader at least a hint that there are other people around. Much as I would love to get through some days without any human interaction – especially when the deadline for this book was looming – it rarely happens, and it would happen even less often for your characters who, unlike me, probably don't sit at a desk in their attic for most of the working day.

You will be familiar with the concept of extras in a movie or TV show, background actors who help to fill a scene. They are there to make this entirely artificial and fictional scene look real. They are diners in a restaurant, people waiting in a queue, pedestrians strolling by – that sort of thing. In fiction, you don't need to mention and/or describe each person in a location but you can intimate that they are there by mentioning that the bar is crowded, or have your character notice the actions of someone waiting in line with them, or alluding to the noise being made by those around, even overhearing a conversation. Sometimes you will only need a word or two, a sentence at most, to populate your scene but it can make all the difference to making it feel authentic.

Play on your computer

An excellent way to get your head around the concept of world building, the necessity of it, and how it supports a story, is to play any one of the bestselling computer or console games out there at the moment. From violent shoot-'em-ups to cartoon-like adventures, they nearly all rely on a strong fictional world in which the action takes place.

Take *Grand Theft Auto*, for example. This is a hugely successful series of games set in various locations. In each you can select from a range of characters and play as that character through a storyline. How that story unfolds is down to your decisions, actions and digits on the control pad, and the action all takes place in a fictional world that you can see in front of you. One key to the success of the series is that the world it inhabits feels real. It makes logical sense. The buildings look right. The people wear appropriate clothes and act in a way that seems authentic given the circumstances, even if that means stealing a car to get away from the police.

When playing the game, you, as the player, are concentrating on the character you are controlling, or the car you are driving, or the mission you have accepted, and you are able to do that because the stuff going on around you doesn't jar. Try sitting beside someone while they play this sort of game and, instead of watching their character joyride their way through Las Vegas, look around them at the scenery, the landscape, the architecture, the decor, the bystanders and listen to the sounds. What have the creators included to make this world seem real? You will notice that much of it has no part to play in the game itself, it is just there to make things authentic.

And you need to consider this sort of approach when creating the fictional world of your book.

Consider the senses

We have five senses – sight, taste, smell, hearing and touch – and a common mistake when authors write a scene is that they only consider the first of these. You do not need to bombard us with all five all the time, but do think about which one or two would be dominant at any particular time. A food market in a fantasy novel, or indeed in any novel, would be an opportunity to introduce smells and sounds to your description, or to remark upon your character's reaction to them. Don't always tell us what something looks like.

A question of perspective

Some aspects of your fictional world may be fixed and concrete – the location of a building or a town, the social hierarchy, religion, laws and customs – and therefore will not change during your story. They stay the same throughout. But that does not mean that every character views them in the same way.

Again, to take a very basic and contemporary example: I don't like coffee. I just don't like the taste. So, obviously, I never drink it. But I also don't really know the difference between a flat white and an Americano[10], and I rarely frequent coffee shops. And yet most people, as far as I can

---

10   I don't advise asking me to make you a coffee, should the situation ever arise.

tell, pop into coffee shops every day and have very specific and, to them, important requirements as to how their coffee is made. Here we have one major element of our 21st-century culture and it is important not to take for granted that everyone feels the same way about it.

It is easier to see this when you consider something like politics or religion, where people have widely differing views and beliefs, often based on their upbringing, location and circumstances. You wouldn't dream of populating your world with people who all vote for the same political party, but make sure you also consider other things that make up your world and think about how your characters will relate to them and feel about them.

Leave most of it out

Having encouraged you to draw maps, think about smells, consider different perspectives, watch computer games and do plenty of research, I am now going to instruct you to leave most of it off the page. A huge part of world building is creating the fictional landscape – physical, cultural, spiritual and emotional – in your head. If you get a really good fix on this stuff then it will naturally pervade your narrative. Sure, you need to sprinkle the text with sufficient content to bring the world to life but you do not need to overload us. Your book is first and foremost about the story. Do not smother the story with too much detail. Be subtle and your novel will benefit from that.

Check for consistency

Don't worry about this too much in your early drafts but once you move into editing or rewriting mode it is good to take a step back and read your story with an eye on how consistent you have been with the many aspects of world building you have included. From something simple, such as a particular building always being in the same place, to less tangible elements like weather, religion, attitudes, social structure.

As I said at the start of this chapter, the depth of world building required will very much depend on the type of book you are writing, but creating a believable world for your story and characters to inhabit is essential for all novels.

8

Plot

The importance of plot within your book will depend on the type of story you are writing. A crime novel, especially a whodunnit, is massively reliant on plot – who does what, when they do it, why they do it and what the consequences are. A lyrical, poetic novel that lingers on mood, scenery and emotion may not have much of a plot driving the action, if indeed there is any action. But, generally speaking, all novels have some sort of plot and, as with most aspects of writing, there are mistakes and pitfalls that are best avoided when creating your plot, as well as strategies for keeping on top of it.

Plotters vs Pantsers

There are two broad schools of writing when it comes to plot – Plotters and Pantsers. A Plotter is someone who prefers to plan out their novel in advance, to have almost a full plot in place and a guideline to follow as they write. A Pantser, as the name suggests, writes by the seat of their pants and sees where the story and characters take them. There are advantages and disadvantages to each, and you can view it as a sliding scale, with some authors at the extreme ends but most at some point in between.

Pantsers often put their characters into a situation and then have to find ways to write them out of it. They do so in ways that feel logical given the person, place and time they are writing about. This often adds authenticity to the story and helps readers believe what is going on. However, it can take time for the logical steps to unwind and Pantsers are often the authors of long books. George RR Martin is definitely a Pantser.

Plotters know what is going to happen before they write it and that, more often than not, allows for a swift, page-turning read. But it can also lack spontaneity or, at times, the plot can seem to be driving the story, losing a bit of authenticity as it does so.

Neither method is better than the other, it just depends what works for you. You may find that you are quite adaptable and can turn your hand to either method depending on what is needed, or you might naturally fall into one camp and only feel comfortable working that way. So what is your point, Scott? Essentially, I just want you to be aware of this theory and that you don't feel there is only one way to tackle plot. Find the approach that you feel most comfortable with and then see if it helps you produce good work.

Because Pantsers tend to get stuck in, the following advice may be more suitable to Plotters, but try to get through the next few pages no matter which camp you want to plant your flag in.

The Spike Lee method

When writing and directing his early feature films (I don't know if he still does it), Spike Lee would summarise each scene on an index card and keep them in an index file box. That way he could make notes on each scene separately, move them around, temporarily or permanently remove them, or stick them back in. The point is that he had notes, thoughts and ideas on each scene, and viewed his stories as a *collection* of scenes. It can work particularly well when you want to try out a re-ordering of scenes, or for discovering whether the removal of a scene will affect the overall plot.

You can do it with actual index cards in an actual box, or you can replicate it with software. Scrivener, a popular piece of software for writers, has an index-card layout on screen, if you want to use it. Some authors do something similar with post-it notes on a wall, or cards pinned onto a cork board. The actual method will depend on your circumstances but the idea of creating a flexible catalogue of scenes is a good one to consider when creating your plot.

Write a synopsis

As you will see when you reach the chapter on perfecting your submissions, writing a synopsis after a book is written is a massive pain in the arse. So it may help to start one early. If you have much of the story and plot in your head then get it down on paper, even if you expect it to change. Sometimes just writing out the sequence of events will flag up plot holes, inconsistencies or other things that need attention. You don't need to fix them at this stage, but it is good to be aware of them. Also, having a document you can refer back to while writing and amend while you go along can be a useful anchor, a way to stay close to your original idea, or sense-check any detours or changes. Will this work? Let's check the synopsis and see.

Don't make it obvious

Your plot needs to be bubbling away under the surface of the story, not popping its head up or somersaulting out of the water like some sort of performing dolphin. We all know there is a plot going on, but we don't want it to be obvious. One common note I make when editing books for which plot is important, such as a crime novel, is to point out when it is blatant that something is happening just because the author needs it to happen for their plot. If the only reason for a character to act in a certain way, or for a particular event to take place, is because your plot needs it to, then it will usually stand out as clunky. (In fact, I tend to write CLUNK in the margins when editing a book where this happens.)

Give some thought to how you can create a situation or a character motivation that seems authentic. Need your heroine to visit a particular room? Give her a reason to do so that makes sense. Important that two characters meet at a particular point in the plot? Ensure it doesn't feel contrived.

Action/reaction

For every action there is an equal and opposite reaction. What is true of physics is true of storytelling. We may not be able to see the reaction every time but you, as the writer, need to consider it. Everything has consequences, even if they are minor and insignificant. If a bomb goes off, literally or figuratively, then the characters and events in your book need to react accordingly, and the consequences need to be felt.

Fill the plot holes

When editing manuscripts, I often finding myself pointing out plot holes. How did she get there? Why would he know about this? Didn't that character leave the room ten pages ago? Believe me, your reader will notice when something doesn't make sense. Recently I read a hugely enjoyable book by a writer I admire but there were a few really obvious plot holes and continuity errors. At first I thought it was just me being overly picky, reading the book as an editor rather than a reader, but when I checked the reviews on Amazon, well over half of them mentioned the same problems. They really do get noticed.

Chances are you won't have the answer for every little plot issue in your first draft, and that is fine, as long as you make a note of them. Be aware of what doesn't quite work and make sure you address it before the final draft.

9

Show vs Tell

If you have read any other books or online articles about writing, the chances are that at some point you have been told: 'show, don't tell'. It is a common piece of advice that is often viewed as a cast-iron rule of writing.

Put simply, the idea is that it is more effective to show the reader something and let them work out what is going on than to tell them outright. The revered short-story writer, Chekhov, has a great line that illustrates the point:

Don't tell me the moon is shining; show me the glint of light on broken glass.

And, in general, this is pretty good advice. Readers tend to be a sophisticated bunch and they can glean most of what they need to know from a story without it being spelled out for them. However, I am always wary of any writing advice that is presented as definitive and hopefully within this book I have offered a range of options because, quite frankly, every writer, every reader and every book is different and if everyone stuck to the rules then literature would be predictable and boring. However, it is useful to know why 'rules' such as Show, Don't Tell have proliferated.

When you read a novel you are discovering a new world, a fictional world created by the author, and part of that experience is immersing yourself in that world and finding your way around. A novel that is all telling and no showing is more like a guided tour than an immersive experience and most readers would find that less rewarding. On the other hand, a novel where everything is inferred or implied can come across as a bit vague, and less grounded. Balance is the key. It is a good idea to do more showing than telling, but don't feel pressured to do that all the time.

Let's take a simple example. One of your characters is upset. You could just write *Sheila was upset* and be done with it. You've put the information across, the reader knows Sheila is upset, let's crack on. However, it would be fair to say that is a pretty lazy and unsophisticated method of conveying emotion, especially when there are many other ways of doing it. You can let us into Sheila's thoughts so that we understand what she is thinking, you can describe her body language, mention that she is trying to hold back tears, put words in her mouth that show us what she is feeling rather than telling us – and those are just four of many possible options.

The same with description. *The pub was crowded* does

enough to make us picture a crowded pub. Good work, take the rest of the day off. However, having your character push through a sea of bodies to get to the bar, needing to raise their voice to place an order and spilling some of the drinks on the way back are, I would argue, more interesting ways of getting that across.

But there are times when it is much better to tell the reader what has happened rather than spend several sentences or paragraphs showing them.

If a character is taking a plane from country A to country B, we don't need to see everything that happens during the flight unless it has an important part to play in the story. You can just tell us that they flew from London to New York, perhaps mentioning that it was an uneventful trip.

The same for passages of time. *Two weeks passed* is perfectly acceptable if we need to get to that point in the story. *It was three years before he saw her again* is also fine. Like I said earlier, balance is the key. Use an appropriate method for the part of the story you are writing, mix it up by all means, but over-reliance on one style can make for a less than engaging read.

10

Classic Mistakes

As part of my research for this book I looked back through dozens upon dozens of edits and editorial assessments I have performed over the years, and I found I was picking out the same mistakes in manuscripts time and time again. I have covered many of these in the chapters you have just been reading but here are a load more that don't really fit into any of the previous sections.

Use of capitals

There is a tendency to use an initial capital for words that really do not need them. The days of the week need initial capitals – Monday would look odd without one – as do the months of the year (my birthday is in November if you want to check out my wish-list on Amazon), but seasons do not. It is spring, summer, autumn and winter, not, however much you want them to be, Spring, Summer, Autumn and Winter.

Likewise with occupations. An accountant is not an Accountant.

Relations and their titles can be confusing. Usually an aunt is just an aunt, even if she is *your* aunt, but when referring to her by name she can be Aunt Jessica, as that is her 'title'. A reasonable rule of thumb is to avoid capitals unless the title is alongside a person's name, or if a character is addressing someone directly.

'My dad taught at my school,' said Scott is correct. No need to write it as Dad.

'Hey, Dad, I wish you didn't teach at my school,' said Scott is also correct. I am directly addressing my dad.

The same goes for doctor/Doctor[11], detective/Detective major/Major, (and other ranks in armed forces or the police).

Acronyms and abbreviations

Generally speaking we don't use full stops or periods when writing acronyms. This is to avoid a text littered with dots. United Nations becomes UN not U.N., and the British Broadcasting Corporation becomes BBC, not B.B.C., for example. You may notice how the full stop followed by a

---

11   Can't you see I'm burning, burning?

comma looks a bit awkward in that previous sentence, and this is avoided by omitting the dots.

We also leave them out for some abbreviations: Mrs is used rather than Mrs., and Dr rather than Dr.. And look at that horrible double dot! However, every publisher has its own style guide. You do not need to worry too much about all of this, but it is useful to know and a good habit to get into.

It is all a bit tense

I am not here to teach you grammar from scratch but I do want to flag up the number of times that I notice changes in tense during a book, even during a short passage. If a story is being told in the past tense then it is best to stick to that within a scene or chapter. If you want to write different scenes, different chapters or different narrators in another tense then that is OK but there needs to be a clear change in scene, using a separator or new chapter to indicate that, otherwise it is confusing to the reader. Sometimes I work with writers who have problems with tenses – it is just something they get wrong no matter how hard they try – and if that is the case with you then just make sure you are aware of it and get an editor to check your manuscript before you send it off.

Names and pronouns

Overuse of a character's name is a common error I find in manuscripts. Scott did this, Scott did that, Scott jumped over here, Scott fell down there, Scott muttered to himself that he was a clumsy bastard. Once you have established which character you are talking about, you don't need to mention their name every time; whole paragraphs can go by with just pronouns – he, she, they – as long as there is no confusion about who is doing what. Scenes involving multiple characters will, understandably, require a more frequent use of names but even there, if it is obvious who you are talking about, a pronoun is just fine.

And do bear in mind that we live in a world where not everyone refers to themselves as 'he' or 'she'. 'They' and 'them' are the preferred pronouns for people who do not identify as male or female and they are pronouns that everyone uses when talking more generically or when the gender of a person is unclear:

> *'Dad, there's someone at the door.'*
> *'What do they want?'*

Even people who claim to be against non-gendered pronouns will find they use them all the bloody time anyway (see above).

A few words about...

Many of you will know the information I am about to share with you, but this stuff is not routinely taught in schools these days and this is apparent from the number of manuscripts I read and edit that get it wrong.

Every word on this page, so far, has been printed in normal standard text. *But this sentence is in a slanty, slightly different text.* The formal name for this sort of standard text is 'roman'. *The name for this sort of slanty text is 'italic'.*

Roman text is used most of the time in pretty much all books. It is the standard, default way of presenting words on a page. Italics are used when you want to make a word stand out, or to highlight it in some way. Here are the most common uses of italics:

Emphasis. When you want a single word, or a few words, within a sentence to have more stress on them that the others. So, a phrase such as:

He was the love of my life

reads differently to:

He was *the* love of my life.

As a reader you automatically stress the word 'the' in the second sentence. Italics can be very useful in fiction when you are writing dialogue, and in non-fiction when you need to ensure the reader reads your sentence in a certain way.

Italics are also traditionally employed when using a word or phrase that is not common in the English language, such as:

The dish had a certain *je ne sais quoi*. I'll never forget it.

Here the italics just alert the reader to the fact that these words are to be read differently. There is no hard and fast rule regarding when and how to use them for non-English words, but generally you'd go for italics when the words are not common. You wouldn't use them for croissant or siesta. You would almost certainly use italics for *mzee* (an East African tribal elder) and *kathak* (an Indian dance form). Whether to use them for café au lait or vaporetto is up to the writer and I can't imagine any readers getting too upset by either option.

Italics are also used for the titles of books, films, albums, newspapers, magazines and plays when they appear in the main body of a text. But it is important to note that the titles of songs, poems and short stories are presented within inverted commas. So the following would be correct:

I was reading *The Hitch-Hiker's Guide to the Galaxy* when 'Paranoid Android' suddenly came on the radio.

And neither italics *nor* inverted commas (see what I did there?) are used for brand names or the names of shops or restaurants.

To be honest, all of this would be picked up by an editor, but as an editor who is constantly having to fart around fixing this sort of thing, I feel it is my duty to pass it on.

...italics

TMI

Too much information. Specifically, avoid info dumps. Giving a detailed list of the technical capabilities of a fighter plane the moment it is mentioned in your thriller is an info dump. Outlining the history of an ancient building as your character walks into it to meet their one true love is an info dump. Sharing the full financial background of a corporation that plays a role in your spy novel is an info dump.

If you need the reader to be aware of a piece of information, then think about how to share that – and even whether you need to share it at all. A sprinkling of information within the narrative is fine, but a paragraph or more is usually overdoing it. Perhaps one character can ask a question of another, or you can reveal the information gradually. If you really must share shitloads of information in one go then you could frame it as a news report or something like that but, in general, info provided all at once in a big torrent is rarely fun to read.

Redundancy

As a writer you are just as free to employ a verbose, ornate style as you are to be economical and spare with your words. But however florid your style, it really is a good idea to avoid saying the same thing twice, especially in the same sentence.

'I am furious about this,' screamed Scott, angrily.

Three times, there. If a character says something that makes it obvious they are angry then you don't need to point out they are doing so *angrily*. And screaming is usually a good indicator of anger, fear or annoyance. Anyway, at least one of the three is redundant, and probably two.

Redundant language refers to any words that add nothing to your script – often because the information they impart has already been shared with the reader or is of no real benefit to them. Keep an eye out for this as it happens a fair bit.[12]

Body language

So, here's a thing, people rarely do the things with their bodies that novelists make their characters do. Running their fingers through their hair, dropping their jaws in surprise, having a shiver run up their spine. These are all things that happen way more often in fiction than they do in real life. I have come to realise that authors just really like describing what a character is doing and find it a useful shorthand to show emotions and temperament, especially when trying to show rather than tell. And that is fine as long as it feels authentic, but most of these common actions end up as

---

12   An excellent example flagged up by one of my beta readers, Kat, is the redundant use of 'sense' as a shorthand for, as she calls it, 'something I can't quite bother to describe better'. He sensed rather than saw a figure – sight is a sense, in fact. The smell filled her senses – what does that even mean?

clichés and we have already discussed why clichés are not a good thing in the main. I often advise authors to invest in a book about body language, or to watch some good online videos, to see what people really do with their bodies when they are scared, thoughtful, anxious, and so on.

Two spaces after a full stop

Or period, if you are of a North American persuasion. I occasionally tweet writing and editing advice on Twitter and this subject prompts more ire than almost any other. There are lots of ardent two spaces advocates who are, of course, very welcome to their opinion. Even if they are wrong.

Another history lesson for you here, you lucky blighters. Many of us were taught to put two spaces after a full stop when typing any sort of document. At least, we were if we grew up in the day when typewriters proliferated but that is no longer the case. Actually, it wasn't the case before typewriters either. Typographers of old went to great lengths to ensure that the printed word was crisp, clear and readable. To achieve this they developed a system of proportional type where wide letters took up more space than thin letters, reflecting the way they tended to look when written down by hand – an 'M' is wider than an 'I'. Then typewriters came along and really buggered things up. You see, manual typewriters use monospaced type in which every letter and symbol is the same width. This is vital to ensure that they actually work and the keys don't stick all the time but one side-effect was that you needed to leave two spaces after a full stop for anyone to actually notice it was there. The need for monospaced type died out in the 1970s when computers and electric typewriters invaded the office space. Proportional type was restored. But generations of people had grown up with the two-space rule, and the double space abounds to this day, albeit with slowly declining frequency. It simply isn't needed any more.

Does it matter? It certainly isn't something that will damage your chances of publication but, you know, if you fancy embracing the world post-1980 then maybe it is worth making that bold move into a double-space-free life. It will certainly help copyeditors who spend far more time than is necessary removing double spaces from manuscripts written by authors aged 50-plus.

Words and music

If you intend to quote any song lyrics, poetry or lines from plays or movies or books in your novel then you need permission to do so. Think about it; you are using someone else's words. It is only polite to check this is OK with them. You'd want the same courtesy shown to you, I am sure. Sometimes the rights owner is happy for the work to be used for free but usually a payment is expected, and a credit is essential in either case. But be warned, it can be bloody hard to get permission, and also expensive. It is often best to avoid the use of other people's work, perhaps making reference to it obliquely instead.

Titles are fine. You can mention that someone is dancing to 'Where Is My Mind?' by Pixies, but just don't quote the lyrics.

The exception tends to be with non-fiction, when the work is a critical study or review. A chapter in a book about popular culture that looks at the use of 'Where Is My Mind?' at the end of the film *Fight Club* might refer to the way certain events happen while certain lyrics are being sung. That would be OK.

Hopefully you won't be guilty of too many of these minor crimes, but at least we've covered them now so you won't get arrested by the grammar police any time soon.

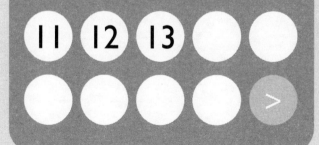

Revising
Your
Book

I regularly get approached by authors – some looking for me to edit their work and others submitting to me for potential publication – who have clearly only typed THE END on their first draft a few days ago. And while they may well have completed a pretty good draft, they have not made any attempt to revise, rewrite or edit it. The act of getting the words down on the page is only one part of the writing process. As Ernest Hemingway once said, 'The only kind of writing is re-writing.' He also said, 'The first draft of anything is shit.' I may not agree with everything he said but he was pretty accurate with those two nuggets of wisdom.

If you really want to make it in the book world, if you want to write a bestseller or win a literary award or be read by a loyal band of faithful fans, then you need to learn how to rewrite, how to go back to the stuff that you have typed and make it better. This chapter looks at some of the ways you can do just that.

11

The Art of Rewriting

So you have finished the first, or latest, draft of your book. Congratulations, that is quite a feat. You deserve a break. Seriously – take some time off. It will do you, and your manuscript, the world of good if you put some time and distance between each other. I would recommend leaving it a couple of weeks before you dive back in, but I know many of you will be too impatient for that. Try to give it a few days, at least, if at all possible.

There are lots of reasons for taking this approach. When you finish a draft you will already be aware of the things that need fixing or parts of the book that require attention, but by pausing for a while you enable yourself to think through those issues a bit more, allowing them to settle and solutions to develop. We all know the concept of sleeping on something – going to bed before making a big decision the next day – and this is much the same thing, but ideally over a longer period. You also need to change mode. If this is a first draft then you will have been on writing mode for months. You now need to shift to revising mode and a forced break helps to make that leap. What's more – and this is the reason I find most compelling – you have a more objective view on a piece of writing if some time has passed since you wrote it. When I flick through some of my early books I am equally impressed by certain passages of prose – 'I can't remember writing that but it is actually pretty good' – and appalled by the clunkiness of others, finally seeing the problem and solution to a difficult section but, sadly, years too late.

The advice above is more or less universal – a rarity in this book. I genuinely feel most writers would benefit from a break between drafts. How you tackle rewrites and revisions will depend on your own style and tastes and attitude to writing, but what follows might be of help.

Make a list as you go along

While you are writing your book you will undoubtedly come across passages that don't feel quite right, or realise there is a problem with a character or plot point, but you don't have a solution just yet so you get on with the writing. This may seem like an obvious thing, but write each issue down as you go. If you do this you will have a pretty comprehensive To Do list when you get to the end of your draft. You can then address this list using one or more of the following strategies. Or one of your own.

One thing at a time

When I am working with an author I usually advise them to tackle one issue at a time. If your list of things to do includes tightening the dialogue, fleshing out certain characters, reining back the adverbs, and solving some plot holes then there is no need to go to page one and work your way through chronologically, fixing each thing as it crops up. Instead, pick one issue and concentrate on that.

Let's say it is dialogue. You know you want to make it more authentic and ensure that each character has their own vocal style and rhythm. Great. Make your way through the book and each time you hit some dialogue, have a crack at making it better. If you come across some adverbs or a plot hole while you are doing this, ignore them. You are not here to sort those out yet.

The benefits to this approach are that you can really get under the skin of one particular issue, you can stay consistent because you are focusing on that one thing, and you have the satisfaction of completing a task rather than having lots of tasks on the go at once. But perhaps the biggest benefit of all is that it breaks down what might seem like a huge job into smaller, more manageable chunks.

You can then, obviously, go back and tackle the next issue, then the next. I refer to it as rewriting in waves, one at a time.

Once you have addressed each issue it can be a good idea to go through the whole manuscript again and make notes of where you think there is still room for improvement.

You are a better writer now than you were then

If you have spent a year writing your book then you have had a year's more experience as a writer when you type THE END than when you typed CHAPTER ONE. So perhaps you want to focus your initial attention on the parts of the book you wrote before you had all that experience. You may be surprised to see how many mistakes you were making back then. And if you have not written your book in chronological order, check out the passages you wrote early on, no matter where they appear in the book.

What does your draft need?

An early draft can be a reasonably complete story that requires some revision or tweaking, or it can be a very rough outline that needs a lot more fleshing out, a lot more writing, and a lot more thinking before it becomes anything resembling an actual book. And there are lots of stages in between.

Different types of draft need different approaches to

rewrites. Take some time to really think about what you need. Is this a tweaking and patching-up job, or is it a substantial period of new writing to build upon a rough framework? Draw up your strategy accordingly.

Don't go with your first idea

If you have an issue that you need to resolve then you'll probably spend some time thinking of a solution. My challenge to you is not to automatically go with the first solution you come up with. Initial ideas are often the obvious ones and the first thing that springs to mind is less likely to be original. Force yourself to come up with one or two additional solutions. You may not end up using them every time but it will take you out of your comfort zone, help you avoid lazy thinking, and may, from time to time, be the difference between a good piece of writing and a great piece of writing.

Get a second opinion

Once you feel your book is taking shape and is some way towards resembling the story you plan to send out in the world, it might be time to get someone else to read it. This may not be an appropriate action until draft five or ten or twenty, but getting a fresh pair of eyes on your work can be hugely beneficial.

Now, I don't mean to offend anyone here, but when selecting someone to read your work it is best to avoid loved ones, close friends, and family, unless they have some sort of experience in the book world. These people love you and care for you, so are less likely to tell you which bits of your book don't work. They are predisposed to supporting you and encouraging you. What you really need is a good, constructive critic. You may know another writer you can ask, and to whom you can return the favour, or someone in your social network who is an avid reader with strong opinions. You may choose to employ a professional[13] to read and offer an assessment of your draft. However you go about it, find someone who will be as objective as possible.

You then need to consider the feedback they give. With luck, their views will broadly agree with yours – the characters or scenes you were concerned about are ones they don't think quite work – and that gives you reassurance that your planned rewrites are on the right track. If they don't like something that you consider to be a crucial part of your book then you may want to ignore them, but do at least consider the feedback. And, importantly, if more than one person takes issue with the same aspect of the book, that is a very good sign that you need to address it.

---

13   Full disclosure: This is something I do to pay the bills. I read manuscript drafts and tell authors what is wrong, and right, with them and offer advice on next steps. You can hire me if you want – you can find more information about this in the Resources section at the end of the book – but don't feel obliged

Go with your gut

I mention this later in the book as well, but I often give feedback to authors only to hear, 'Ahh, yes, I knew that was a problem.' Now, that is fine and dandy, and I am glad they were aware of the issue, but they have just paid me to tell them something they already know. I realise that confirmation can often be as useful as that initial recognition, but my point is that you probably already know what the problems are with your manuscript. Do not ignore that gut feeling. If you sense that something is wrong, try to fix it.

Deletion is not failure

You will have to delete words, sentences, scenes, perhaps even entire characters (RIP) when revising and rewriting your book, but this is a good thing and it does not mean those words, sentences, scenes, and characters were wasted. They needed to be there so that you could see the overall shape of the book, so that you could find out what worked and what didn't; the removal of them is as much a part of the writing process as putting the words on the page in the first place.

Although, actually, don't delete anything…

Reuse and recycle

When I talk about deletion I mean the removal of content from one draft to improve the next. In reality, you need to save copies of all your drafts as you never know when something might come in useful. You may have removed a scene in draft two, but the rewrites in subsequent drafts mean that it is needed again and you can go back and salvage it.

Likewise, just because some writing is cut from your manuscript it doesn't mean the writing is bad and can't be used again. Some of your finest sentences or scenes may have to be removed for the greater good of the current manuscript, but that doesn't stop you from using them at some point in the future, even in a completely different book. Nothing goes to waste. Douglas Adams used to recycle deleted scenes and storylines all the time. Heck, the first *Dirk Gently* book is basically a ditched *Doctor Who* script re-written in novel form.

You'll need to do this more than once

It is highly unlikely that you'll get everything sorted in one set of rewrites, and that is fine. You may need to go back through your manuscript several times; you may end up with multiple drafts. It is all part of the process. If you found one or more of the ideas above helpful, repeat them with each draft. Pause for a while between each draft, but keep going. You will get there in the end.

Let it go

At some point you need to stop. Ask yourself: Is this as good as I can make it? If so, then it might be time to release it into the world and see what others think.

The rewriting and revision process is a vital part of writing a book, but it employs slightly different techniques from those you will have used when creating that first draft. Rewriting and writing are separate skills, albeit closely related, and need to be viewed as such. This may be an area where you need the help of a professional, but hopefully the advice above will help keep you on track as you chip away at your early drafts and turn them into a finished book.

12

Editing Your Book

Revising, which we have just covered, is all about going back over your manuscript and making substantive changes; tweaking and rewriting it until you feel the story and storytelling is as strong as possible. It may involve scrapping whole sections, creating lots of new content, playing around with the order of scenes, improving aspects such as dialogue or description – all manner of important things to make your story work. Rewriting is about changes to the story itself and how it is told, and is always performed by the author of the text.

Editing comes afterwards – once the story is written and considered more or less complete – and, in the main, it focuses much more on the structure of the writing than the story. It is often performed by someone other than the author, a person handily known as an editor.

Types of edit

There are, broadly speaking, three types of edit and they are usually performed in this order:

Structural edit
Also known as a developmental edit, this is where an editor reads your manuscript and comments on the story itself – what works, what doesn't, is the twist too obvious, is the pacing right, does it all make sense, which areas could be improved and how. It also focuses on many of the key aspects we have covered in this book, such as dialogue, character, and world-building. The end result would normally be an annotated version of your manuscript along with a report or series of notes, which you can use to improve your book. A structural edit will often prompt another round of rewrites and revises. This is the sort of edit I do to pay my bills until this book sells millions and I can retire to my country pile.

Copyedit
This is a correctional edit, with the editor checking the text for any errors. A copyedit would pick up typos, punctuation and grammar issues, and flag up ambiguous writing or any inconsistencies in the story. A copyeditor is making sure there is nothing technically wrong with the text. They possess an in-depth knowledge of grammar and how the English language works. I leave this sort of edit to the pedants.

Proofread

A proofread only happens once a book is typeset and ready to be printed, and it is a final check of the text to correct any typos or layout issues.

If you are following the traditional publishing route then all of the above edits will have been organised by your publisher and performed by other people, not you. If you are self-publishing then I strongly recommend that you invest in a professional editor to do this work for you. Your budget may not stretch to paying three separate people to do the three different edits, but if you publish your book without either a structural edit or a copyedit you really are asking for trouble. I cover this in more detail in the forthcoming chapter on self-publishing.

If, however, you are determined to edit your own work then the following chapter offers some tips and advice.

13

How to Edit
Your Own Work

When editing your own work it is useful to create some distance from yourself and the *story* because this next phase is all about the *text*. You are looking for errors, inconsistencies, and problems, and these are easy to miss if you get swept up in the narrative and lost in the story itself. What follows are some strategies to help you take a few steps back and view your text in an objective manner when copyediting and proofreading. Some of these, inevitably, overlap with the content of the chapter on rewrites, but I am leaving them here in case you are reading this chapter in isolation, or returning to it while editing your work. It is unlikely that all of these will be of use to you, but one or two might prove to be techniques you can employ. Also, it isn't a good idea to do several of these at the same time. Pick one approach and apply that to your manuscript. Once complete, select another and go back to your book with that. Each strategy will help you spot, highlight, and fix different issues in your work, so choose the ones that you feel will be most helpful for you.

Walk away

There's a lot to be said for the humble desk drawer or, more accurately in this digital age, the unopened computer folder. Once you have typed THE END, leave your manuscript alone for a while – at least a few days but ideally a week or more – so that you can come at it fresh with your editing hat on[14]. I can guarantee that you will spot issues you would otherwise have missed if you had dived straight in.

You already know all this

Chances are you already know what the problems are with your work. Before you start rewriting or editing, take some time to write down all your concerns. Which bits of the book don't spark joy?[15] Are there any plot points that feel unresolved to you? Is there a character that you are worried isn't fleshed out enough? Do you have any bad writing habits that could have crept into the manuscript? By writing

---

14   An actual hat is not compulsory but be my guest if you fancy giving it a go.

15   Sorry, I couldn't resist.

down your concerns you will cement them in your mind and when you come to re-read or edit you will be on the lookout for them.

Word cloud

For the uninitiated, a word cloud is an online tool that allows you to input a chunk of text, after which it spews out a handy graphic showing all the words within that text with the most common words bigger and bolder than the rest. For example, here is a word cloud for the book you are reading now.

Unsurprisingly, perhaps, the word BOOK is the most prominent, and it is nice to see CAN big and bold, as that suggests there is a bit of a positive vibe flowing through the book, but quite why the word ONE was so large baffled me.

When you run *your* word cloud, you would expect to see common words – and, the, she, he, said, the names of your characters – appear in big font, and that is fair enough as they are functional words that your manuscript needs to make sense. What you want to watch out for are the unexpected or unusual words that loom large and bold, words that you didn't realise you use frequently. Perhaps you are a serial 'suddenly' user, or overly fond of 'actually', or find yourself typing a seemingly random word much more often than you expected. I certainly had a look through my manuscript to see why ONE was cropping up so frequently. Whatever your word cloud throws up, it is a simple and effective way to highlight the overuse of certain words, or the unusually frequent use of others, and should prompt a few changes in your manuscript.

We all get better with age

Writing a book takes time, usually several months or even years. And, like most things in life, the more you do something the better you get at it. You are almost certainly a better writer now than you were when you started your book. So why not revisit the parts you wrote first and ask yourself if you would write them the same way today? If you wrote your book in chronological order, taking your plot from start to finish, your progress as a writer can be even more pronounced when reading the book back. Quite often when I edit a book for a client I find far more issues in the opening chapters than the closing ones and it is abundantly clear that their writing and storytelling has improved in between the writing of them.

Show vs tell

Your readers are intelligent people. They read books. They can fill in the gaps. You really don't have to tell them everything. They'll work it out.

I have covered show vs tell in more detail elsewhere, but it is worth reminding you about it here. When re-reading your book, make a note of the sections where you tell the reader something and challenge yourself with this simple question: Could I show them this instead? The answer won't always be 'yes', but when it is, consider revising that passage or scene.

You're fired!

We have covered the use of redundant language and phrases earlier in this book. Read through your work on the lookout for redundancies. If you've said it once you usually don't need to say it again.

Feeling tense

It is not unusual for tenses to change as you write. You may have begun your book in the present tense but later decided the past tense was better. Even if you have gone through changing present to past you may have missed some instances. Some writers flit between tenses entirely unknowingly. Whatever the reason, I often see this in the edits I am paid to perform, and giving your book a read through with an eye on incorrect tense is a very good idea.

Get your ruler out

Do you really need those long sentences? Lengthy, convoluted sentences containing several clauses and asides can be hard for the reader to follow or, perhaps worse, a bit boring to read. This may be a deliberate and conscious part of your writing style, and that is fine, but if that isn't the case then you might want to watch out for any rambling sentences and prune them a little.

Don't worry, this isn't a plea for dumbing down or always keeping things simple. A well-crafted sentence can be a beautiful thing to behold but it is always worth challenging yourself and your writing: does this sentence work the way I want it to? We want readers admiring your writing, not tripping up over it.

Adverb sit-ups

I don't want to get into a big debate about the use of adverbs, but it is fair to suggest that an overuse of them can give your book a slightly amateur feel, as if you are trying a bit too hard to sound 'writerly'. At least, most agents and publishers will be of that opinion, so you might as well accept it.

While editing, make yourself do ten sit-ups every time you come across an adverb. You'll soon start taking some of them out – or you will end up with awesome abs. A win-win situation.

It's the simple stuff, stupid

Check the basics. You have spellcheck; use it. Watch out for homonyms (spellcheck won't find them). Make sure your formatting is consistent. All the obvious stuff, basically. You may be surprised how often this is missed.

Shh, listen

Reading your work aloud is a great way to spot issues and problems. If you find yourself stumbling over certain words, or a particular passage, then the chances are your readers will do the same when reading it in their heads. You will also notice things such as repetition, and typos and punctuation errors will stand out more clearly when you read aloud.

Better still, record yourself (or someone else) reading it and play it back later so you can take notes on the broader aspects of the story. Which sections seemed to drag? Was the pacing fast enough during the action sequences? Are any aspects of the plot confusing?

Reading aloud, and listening to your work, will really test your dialogue-writing skills. If dialogue does not sound authentic when actually spoken then you need to go back in and fix it.

Pretend it is already published

One issue with writing and editing a book is that you are almost always doing so via a medium that is very different to the experience of reading a book. You are probably typing everything into a computer or tablet; you are reading, checking and editing things on screen. Most of us, even in this digital age, read printed books and we do so sitting in an armchair, or while commuting to work or lying in bed – all of which are very different experiences to typing at a keyboard and staring at a back-lit screen. It isn't possible to produce an actual book from your draft manuscript but there are two things you can do relatively easily to fake that book-reading experience.

One is to get the manuscript printed up. Obviously you

can send the whole thing to your home printer, but this would take ages to spew the thing out and you'd be left with a massive pile of pages and the death of twenty trees on your conscience. Instead, give the file to your local print shop – most towns have somewhere that offers printing and photocopying services – and ask them to create an A5 bound copy printed on both sides of the paper. This would give you a spiral-bound 'book' that is a similar size and shape to a traditional printed book. Sure, it will look a bit homemade but the actual reading experience will be similar to reading a book from your bookshelf.

Alternatively, and a lot cheaper, if you have an eReader then you can just send your manuscript to your device.

The point of this exercise is that you will be re-reading your work in a way that is as close to the traditional reading experience as possible, and you can see how your book holds up in that environment. It is a page-turner, for example? It also forces you to view the book in a slightly different way, and any new angle you can take is likely to be helpful as you decide what to tweak, change, delete or add to your manuscript.

Sdrawkcab gnidaer

When proofreading your work, try reading it backwards. I kid you not. Not you kid I.

One of the dangers when checking your work for errors is that it is easy to fall into the habit of 'reading' it, the way you read any text. When reading, our eyes flit across groups of words, our brain taking them in in chunks. We don't actually stop and read each word separately. Also, when you have written and re-written a manuscript several times you become used to it. By reading your manuscript from the last word to the first you are forcing your brain to concentrate on one word at a time and you are more likely to spot mistakes.

Wait till you're finished

Don't try to edit as you go along. That way madness lies. Wait till you have written the whole thing and then you can get stuck in.

The editing process is one of fixing and correcting, making sure everything is right before taking the next step. If you are self-publishing then a strong, robust edit is vital. This is not necessarily the case if you are submitting to an agent or publisher, as they will want to do their own edits, but it would still be worth spending a bit of time looking at your manuscript with an editor's eye to make it as good as possible before you send it off.

Submission
&
Publication

14

How to Perfect Your Submission

During my two decades in the book world, most of which have been spent as a publisher, I have had thousands of manuscripts submitted to me by eager authors, and it never ceases to amaze me how many otherwise intelligent, articulate and sensible people make a complete hash of this process. I see the same mistakes made time and time again.

This chapter of the book is designed with two aims in mind. First, to ensure that you do not make any of those mistakes. Second, to give you the tools you need to prepare the most professional submission possible. If you heed my advice then you stand an excellent chance of getting your work read and seriously considered by agents and publishers.

Now, let's make our way through the submissions process.

Before you send anything...

Are you ready?

You have finished writing your book and you are contemplating sending it out into the world to be bought by, hopefully, lots of eager readers. These days there are many ways of achieving this, and I cover them elsewhere in this book, but the traditional route remains for the author to find an agent or publisher and have them do a lot of the hard work for you. This is the process we are going to examine here so you may want to flick back to the chapters on 'The Life-cycle of a Book' and 'A Writer's Guide to Publishing Models' for a quick refresher before continuing with this chapter.

Up to speed on the way things work? Good, but before you take one step further on your quest to get published it is important that you pause for a moment, take a deep breath and work out if you really want all this hassle.

Take a cold, hard look at yourself

What you are about to do is bloody difficult. What lies ahead for most of you is months, perhaps years, of frustration. It can dent your confidence. It can crush your self-esteem. Your dream may never come true. This can be a soul-destroying experience. Do you have what it takes to get through this? If in doubt, consider other routes, such as privately publishing, or self-publishing. Or even not publishing at all. This process isn't just about how good your book is, it is about how much you want to be a published author and whether or not you are prepared to deal with everything that comes with that. You do not have to go down this road and there is no shame in opting out at any stage.

What are you trying to achieve?

The approach you should take with your submission will differ depending on your hopes and aspirations. If you genuinely believe your work of genius will sell for a million-pound advance then it is pointless approaching smaller agencies or independent publishers. If you have written a technical journal that only one or two specialist publishers would ever be interested in then you are better off approaching them directly and may not need an agent at all. It is worth spending some time thinking about what it is you are trying to achieve and developing a plan to help make that happen.

Who has read your book?

I would urge you not to submit your book until it has been read by at least a small number of qualified people who have offered feedback. People who are not qualified to do this include relatives, loved ones, people you are sleeping with, people you want to sleep with, people you have slept with in the past, people you may want to sleep with in the future. These people, no matter how honest they are in real life, will generally not want to tell you your book is shit or point out your book's flaws, for all sorts of reasons. Ideally you would find someone who knows a good book when they read one, is blunt and direct, has no agenda and would be prepared to spend the time reading your work and making a few notes. The most opinionated person in your book group wouldn't be a bad person to start with.

Ideally you would be able to get someone to read your manuscript at little or no cost, perhaps in exchange for a drink, a box of chocolates or dinner in a fancy restaurant, but if you can't call in a favour or persuade someone to help you out then it is possible to employ a professional. This is one of the services I offer as a freelance editor, for example, and is known as an editorial assessment. Generally, with an assessment, an editor will read your book and create a report that looks at aspects such as plot, character, style, pace, dialogue and the like, as well as pointing out key issues and suggesting ways to resolve them. It should provide you with all you need to go away and get stuck into a rewrite and, hopefully, end up with a version that is suitable for submission. Prices will vary but, depending on the length of the book, an editorial assessment will cost in the region of £500 to £1,000.

So, definitely easier on the pocket to see who you can bribe with a box of Milk Tray.

Is it really ready to send out?

The majority of manuscripts I reject are clearly a couple of drafts short of being ready. Another few months, a bit more work, and they may have stood more chance of making it to the next stage. Often when I offer feedback on a manuscript the author replies with 'I knew that section wasn't quite right, thanks for confirming it for me' or something like that. If they already knew this, why are they submitting for publication? Agents and publishers do not expect your work to be perfect and ready to publish but why not increase your chances by at least getting it to the point where you genuinely think it is as good as it can be, and your advance readers agree?

Can you handle rejection?

The vast majority of you are going to be rejected more than once, perhaps dozens of times. Get used to it. It isn't nice, though, and it can really knock your confidence. How good are you at receiving criticism? You may be surprised by how hard you take a rejection. However philosophical or thick-skinned you may think you are, your 25th rejection for the same book may be one too many. It has happened to a lot of great writers; you may be another of them. Can you hack it?

Research

Once you have decided that you and your book are ready for the submissions process you need to work out who to submit to – which publisher or agent is most likely to fall in love with your book, or is best placed to help you realise your dream – and to do that you are going to have to embark on a bit of research.

One of the top complaints from agents and publishers about the submissions they receive is a lack of research: authors not doing some simple groundwork before submitting. Here are some things you can do to avoid being such an author.

A few words about...

Make no bones about it, rejection is tough. I don't care how thick-skinned or self-assured you are, someone telling you they don't want or like your work is hard to stomach. It may only take you a few seconds to get over it, although it could take weeks or months, but everyone will experience a little knot of frustration or disappointment when their manuscript is rejected.

You are likely to face rejection quite a lot in this industry, and not just when it comes to finding an agent or publisher. You might secure an agent but your book is rejected by editors; you could get published but Waterstones doesn't stock your book; newspaper reviews might be negative: some idiot on Amazon rates your book with one star; many forms of rejection lie ahead.

Rejection is inevitable, so I suggest that a) you get used to it and b) develop a strategy for dealing with it. I don't mean this in a harsh, 'get a grip' kind of way but more with a 'let's get through this' attitude, and it may help to consider that not all rejection is a bad thing.

People often speculate that the agents and publishers who turned down JK Rowling's *Harry Potter* manuscript – and there were dozens who did just that – have spent the rest of their lives regretting the decision. And perhaps they do kick themselves occasionally but the speculation presumes that they would have been the right home for *Harry Potter*, that they would have been able to help make it the global phenomenon that it went on to be – and that just isn't the case. The agent, publisher and editor that Rowling ended up with were the perfect combination for that book at that time. A different combination would have produced a different book with a different cover and different publishing and marketing strategies. I'd like to think the series would still have been a success but there is also a chance there would never have been a series at all if things didn't work out.

Most of us have been in romantic relationships that ended abruptly or sadly and, at the time, we were devastated. *This was the one for me!* Looking back, we might feel that we dodged a bullet, or at least realise that we are better off where we are now. And it can be the same with publishing. A rejection from Agent X today might piss you off but in a year's time, when Agent Y has signed you up and got you a cracking book deal, the disappointment of that initial rejection will be long forgotten.

You need to find the ideal agent and publisher for your work and the price for that may well be a number of rejections along the way. If they get you where you want to be then they are, ultimately, positive things to have experienced. When you get that dreaded email from an agent, don't think 'My book isn't good enough', think 'This agent was not right for me.'

...rejection

Trade press

Spend time getting to know the industry you are attempting to enter. If you are successful then you are effectively taking on a new job, a new career, even if only part-time. You wouldn't turn up for a job interview without having done some research on the company and finding out as much as you can about the work they do and the people they employ, and you need to do the same when submitting your work.

If you are in the UK then read *The Bookseller* magazine, the main trade publication, which is available in print and online editions. There is also *Bookbrunch*, which is an online trade magazine with a daily mail-out, but this is subscription-only. In the US you would want to concentrate on *Publishers Weekly*. In other countries there will be industry-focused websites and resources which a little bit of Googling will sort out for you. Frequent these sites and read them weekly, or even daily if you can. Follow these publications on Twitter or join their pages on Facebook. Do the same with their key journalists. Over time you will learn who the up-and-coming agents, editors and publishers are, who represents or publishes whom, what books have sold for big advances. Understanding the mood of the industry, what appears to be working and what isn't working, will prove helpful in your quest to become a published author yourself.

Agent and publisher websites

If an agent or publisher would welcome your submission then it will say as much on their website. If they are not going out of their way to tell you this then they probably don't want to hear from you. Their website will also hopefully tell you about the authors they represent or publish, who their key staff are, etc. They don't take too long to navigate and you can learn a lot from them.

In general, agents will welcome submissions, and how to submit will be a key feature of their websites. Publishers tend to be less keen on direct submissions, preferring instead to acquire via agents, but there are exceptions.

Acknowledgements pages

When looking for ideas as to where to send your manuscript, the Thank Yous at the beginning or end of published books can be a good start. Most authors will thank their editors (sometimes tricky people to pin down online) and agents. An hour spent browsing through your own bookshelves and jotting down names will be an hour well spent.

Who represents the authors you admire? This is an extension of the previous point but is still worth making. If you consider Author X to be an influence on your work, or that your book would appeal to a similar readership, why not try submitting to their agent? If the agent likes that author's work they might like yours too. A few words of caution, however: if your work is derivative of, or very similar to, Author X then I would not advise this route. Agents don't want copycat authors. Something with the same tone, style or sensibilities is fine; an imitation is not.

Hang out on Twitter

Lots of agents, publishing houses, editors and other publishing professionals are online these days and Twitter is a great way to – quite legitimately – hang out with them and find out what they have to say. Sure, they'll spend lots of time plugging their books and cooing over cute photos of cats, but they will also offer insight into their work. Feel free to interact with them but don't become a stalker. No one likes stalkers. Not even other stalkers. At my classes, when I ask for a show of hands from people who use Twitter, usually only about half of the attendees put their hands up. Now, there are lots of great reasons not to be on Twitter, and I would love to use it less myself, but it is undoubtedly a place where the people who might end up publishing your book are hanging out on a daily basis, so if you are not there among them then you are almost certainly at a disadvantage.

Writers' & Artists' Yearbook

This classic resource is well worth purchasing as it contains contact details for every UK agent and publishing imprint that matters as well as heaps of extra content and essays on all manner of issues relating to the book world. For several years it contained a piece by me all about the craze for blogs being turned into books but then that fad stopped being interesting and they took it out. These days it features an article I wrote about the mathematics of publishing, the numbers behind the scenes in the book world, an extended version of which is included as a chapter in this book. Your purchase of the *Writers' & Artists' Yearbook* is also a tax-deductible expense, so that's nice. The US equivalent is the annual *Writer's Market* publication.

Writers' communities

There is a plethora of online writing forums and communities. Sure, there are lots of trolls and arseholes to be found lurking within them, and cliques of writers can sometimes form and be hard to crack but, in the main, they are useful places to discuss your work. Do spend some time checking them out before diving in, as some will be better-suited to your personality and writing style. There are also, of course, many writing groups in the real world but these do involve having to talk to actual people face-to-face.

Workshops and festivals

Hardly a week goes by without some literary festival in Upper Throtting, or somewhere similar. Not only that, lots of them have workshops, opportunities to hear agents and publishing folk talk about the industry, and other useful content over and above the usual authors droning on about their books. Check out the programmes of festivals near you and see what's occurring. There are also several writer-focused events and many of these will have one-to-one sessions that can be booked with editors and agents. These are, I think, a worthwhile investment of time and money.

Strategy

OK, so you've done your research. Now you need to spend some time planning how you are going to approach the submissions process. If your book finds a home then, from that point on, it will be subject to a strategy at every stage of its life – when your agent submits it to publishers, when your editor pitches it to their publishing team, when the sales department sells the book to retailers, when the marketing and publicity people try to get reviews and media coverage – so you might as well start strategising now.

Create a longlist

While conducting your research you should keep an ongoing list of all the agents and/or publishers you think would be good matches for your book. It is best to do this as you go along and add notes to remind you why they are on the list and about their specific submission requirements. I am a big fan of using a spreadsheet for this process as this can evolve to keep track of your submissions and responses once you start sending your work out there.

Sort into priority order

Once you are happy that you have researched yourself to tears then you can sort your list into priority order. Who is your dream agent, the one you would go with if everyone you sent your work to offered you a contract? They go top of the list. Work your way down from there. This is an important step, especially if you are thinking positively, as you want to give your dream outcome a chance of actually happening. I know of one author who avoided sending his work to his ideal agent as he didn't want to send it to them 'too early'. He ended up getting an offer from one of the other agents and found himself with the dilemma of whether to accept the offer, hold off that agent while he tried his ideal one, or decline the offer and hope his dream agent came through later. OK, so not the worst situation to be in, and better than being rejected, but a bit messy and best avoided. If you have done your research and made sure your submission is ready then there is no problem with approaching your favoured agent first.

Identify your top five or six

It makes sense to send out more than one submission at a time. Agents expect this and do not mind. I would suggest five or six at a go is about right as it spreads your bets to a degree while also keeping things at a manageable level. Rank your entire list so that you are prepared for the next round of submissions if required. If you do get a positive response from one agent, and that leads to a firm offer, then you can either concentrate on that and forget the others, or you can let the other agents know you have an offer and see if that spurs them into action. Another high-class problem to have, if it does crop up.

More research on each

Now to concentrate on your top group. No matter how much research you have done to date, do some more. If you haven't read at least two books represented by each agent, or published by each editor/publisher, then do it now. Check their Twitter feeds. If an opportunity to interact comes up, take it but don't be a weirdo. Find out what books they have sold or acquired recently, take note if they are having a particularly busy time, keep an extra-special eye out for any moans or complaints they have. Sense-check your decision. If you need to call someone at midnight, sobbing because you can't get the ending of your second book right, is this the person you'd want to call?

Personalise your approach
Think about what you want to say to each of the five people on your list. Ideally it will be different for each. You are not sending out a circular or round-robin letter. If you don't have two or three great reasons for sending to that person then they should not be on the list.

Submit
Now you are ready to pull together your submission. Don't even think of sending stuff out until you have addressed all of the above. I mean it.

The submission

And now to the submission package itself. These days most agents will accept submissions via email. They will be expecting the following for a **fiction** submission:

A query letter
We tend to refer to the introductory message that accompanies a submission as a query letter, or cover letter, even though these days, of course, it will usually take the form of an email.

A pitch
A paragraph or two within the query letter or email that tells the recipient what the book is about and, hopefully, gets them excited about it.

A synopsis
A one-page summary of the book and the key plot.

Sample chapters
Usually three sample chapters or a portion from the start of the book.

However, things are slightly different for a **non-fiction** submission. You still need a query letter containing a pitch, and a sample of your writing, but instead of a synopsis you would include:

A book proposal
A page or two that explains the rationale behind the book, why you are the person to write it and who you think the audience might be.

Chapter breakdown
A brief summary of the book, chapter by chapter.

Over the coming pages I look at each of the above elements in more detail but before I do, I need to impart probably the most important piece of advice in this chapter...

READ THE BLOODY GUIDELINES!

Every publisher or agent who welcomes submissions will have some form of guidelines on their website. Read them. Read them and follow them. I would estimate that 30-40% of all the submissions I have ever received ignored one or more of the guidelines. If they want to see three chapters, do not send them four. If they want the first 5,000 words, don't send them 6,000, or 1,000! If they specify a format, font or template, then use it. If your submission does not get read because you ignored submission guidelines then you have only yourself to blame.

Think about it. The guidelines are there because the person receiving your submission gets hundreds, if not thousands, such submissions every year. Going through them is a mammoth task. They are asking you, politely, to follow certain rules in order to make that process easier. Why would you then deliberately ignore that request and make it harder for them? And if you do that, do you really expect them to look upon you and your work kindly?

Query letter

Does the ideal query letter exist?

Accepting that every agent and publisher is different and will have different requirements, likes and dislikes, there probably isn't one truly perfect query letter, but you can write one that avoids all the mistakes that drive agents up the wall, and that's a bloody good start. Of course, as I have said, these days they are query emails, rather than letters, but you get the idea.

Intro
This needs to be personal. Dear Scott, for example. Dear Sirs (it does happen) is impersonal and ignores the fact that men are in the minority in this industry. More than one of my female friends who are agents and publishers will not read past Dear Sirs if they receive an email addressed in that fashion, and rightly so.

About your book
Open with some brief information about your book. 'I am seeking representation for my crime novel, *Where Evil Remains*, which is complete at 85,000 words' is all you need. This helps the recipient enormously as it means they know what they are dealing with from the outset. If they don't represent crime writers, for example, then they do not need to read any further.

Why are you sending it?
Explain why you are sending your submission to this individual. Don't go over the top with flattery, just be honest. There is a reason you have selected them, so tell them. Unless that reason is 'you are the only agent left who hasn't rejected me', in which case I suggest you lie.

The pitch
This is a brief, one-paragraph blurb for your book. It is probably the most important part of your cover letter so there is more detail on this later.

A few words about...

Social media has made a significant impact on the world of publishing in a number of different areas. It has changed the way publishers and retailers promote books to readers and how readers review books and recommend them to each other. It has enabled authors to have a direct relationship with an audience, even before they have published a book.

But it has also heaped undue pressure on emerging writers, many of whom feel they need to have a big social media profile in order to get published. If you are a debut novelist submitting to agents and publishers, they aren't going to be too bothered whether you are on Twitter or not. It could be considered a bonus if you have 100,000 followers but agents and publishers are primarily interested in the story you have written.

It will be seen as more important in some areas. If you are a food writer, for example, evidence that you have cultivated a big audience could really help with your pitch.

Generally speaking, it is a good thing for authors to be available online and to interact with others in the book world. There is a lot to discover and learn and you can make some great connections that way. As a publisher, I reckon 10-20% of the books I have published in recent years have, in some way, come from social media. So do consider getting involved but don't feel it is absolutely essential.

...social media

Comparison

It can help the agent if you are able to compare your manuscript to recent or well-known books to give them an idea of the sort of thing you are sending them. Doing this without sounding like you are bragging is a good idea. Phrases such as 'early readers have said it reminds them of *Gone Girl*' or 'I'd like to think fans of Gillian Flynn would enjoy my book' are good. 'I am confident that I have written the new *Gone Girl*' is not so good.

A bit about you

Agents and publishers do not care if you are married, or whether or not you have kids. They couldn't give a toss about your extensive record collection, love of knitting or your great sense of humour (unless you are pitching a book about the history of vinyl records or guerrilla knitting). Give them basic and relevant information. 'I am a 34-year-old English teacher who works as a police community-support officer in my spare time' does the job perfectly (you can probably write OK and know a bit about how the policing system works).

Keep it to one page

There is no query letter that needs to be more than one page long, or the equivalent if we are talking about an email. I don't care if you disagree.

That's it. That really is it. Nothing else is required in your cover letter. No jokes, no banter, no rambling, nothing.

Here is a template for a query letter, using a completely made-up novel. Feel free to copy it and adapt it for your own use. Please note, if sending to a publisher rather than an agent then the opening line would need to change to something like: I am submitting for your consideration my crime novel...

Dear Scott,

I am seeking representation for my crime novel, Where Evil Remains, *which is complete at 85,000 words.*

I wanted to submit my work to you after seeing you speak at the Winchester Writers' Festival last year. You spoke about the sort of books you were looking for and I felt my novel, which I was in the process of re-drafting at that stage, might just fit the bill.

Where Evil Remains *is a gritty crime novel set in the East End of London. A Land Rover is found parked on some waste ground near to Mile End tube station. The driver and passenger, both men in smart suits, have been killed by single gunshot wounds to the head. When D.I. Susie Baines recognises them as local drug dealers she realises that the list of suspects will be very long indeed. What she doesn't know is that the culprit is a lot closer to home than she thinks.*

I hope that fans of authors such as Peter James and Nicci French would like my book, and early readers have made those sort of comparisons, which is most flattering.

I have been a police community-support officer serving in the East End for the past decade and, although my book is very much a work of fiction, I have used my experience, and the many stories I have heard from my colleagues in the full-time force, to inform my writing.

I attach a synopsis and the first three chapters of the book, as requested in your submission guidelines. If you would like to read the full novel I would be delighted to send it over to you.

Thanks for taking the time to read my work.

Kind regards,

Scott Pack

Classic mistakes

It is easy to make mistakes but it is even easier to avoid them by not being an idiot. Here are some classic mistakes that idiots make all the time.

Spelling the name wrong

My name is Scott, with two Ts. My surname is Pack. Not Park. Or Packer. There are only nine letters in my name, if you can't get them right then I am willing to bet a year's salary that your book is not going to be good enough to get published. Check and double-check the spelling of the name of your recipient. It's just polite.

Typos

Computers all have this splendid spellchecking function. Please use it. Check your cover letter, synopsis and sample chapters for spelling mistakes. Then get someone else to check them. Agents and publishers won't get too upset if the odd typo sneaks in but some submissions are riddled with them, which is just plain sloppy.

Outrageous claims

Your book is not going to sell as well as *Harry Potter*, I can tell you that now, so don't bother claiming it will. Your book is not as good as *Catch-22*, either, so don't make comparisons. What we care about is your story and how well you've written it, not the size of your cojones. Big, bold, outrageous claims suggest an author with either a) unrealistic expectations or b) a massive ego. Both types of authors are best avoided. Of course, once an author has been successfully published and has a few bestsellers under their belt the chances are that they'll develop a massive ego and have unrealistic expectations, bless them, but you are not there yet.

Genres that don't exist

Can I make it clear now that there is no such thing as a 'fiction novel'? I receive several submissions every year for 'fiction novels'. There is such a thing as 'an author who doesn't know what they are talking about' though. Best not define your book as 'unclassifiable' or 'genre-busting' either. Also, a book cannot be a 'crossover hit' until it has been published in one category and then crossed over to another. Think about the departments and sections of a bookshop. Where would your book go? Just call it that.

Rambling nonsense

Keep things brief, polite and personal. Do not ramble on. Do not give us a reason to sigh and regret opening up the email. Do not give us an excuse not to read your synopsis.

Quirky

You may well be hilarious. Your friends and family may think you are hilarious. You may even have written a hilarious book. You do not need to write a hilarious query letter. Funny and quirky are annoying 99% of the time when it comes to submissions. Do not risk it. Also, do not enclose or attach anything other than the requested or required content. No glitter – it has happened.

The pitch

It could be argued that the pitch is the most important part of your submission. It is the first sight the agent or publisher will get of your story, and it is the story that really matters.

Here, as a reminder, is the pitch section of my template letter:

> Where Evil Remains *is a gritty crime novel set in the East End of London. A Land Rover is found parked on some waste ground near to Mile End tube station. The driver and passenger, both men in smart suits, have been killed by single gunshot wounds to the head. When D.I. Susie Baines recognises them as local drug dealers she realises that the list of suspects will be very long indeed. What she doesn't know is that the culprit is a lot closer to home than she thinks.*

And here are some tips to help you achieve something similar with yours.

One paragraph
The pitch should take up one paragraph of your cover letter. Any more and you'll struggle to keep your letter to a single page. You could stretch to two if you were really disciplined about length but do avoid the temptation to witter on too much.

Summarise the book in under 100 words
Here's a tip. Try summarising a few classic books, or some of your favourite books, in no more than 50 words. It can be done and is great practice for your own pitch. The word-count is not a strict rule, by any means, but is a good target to aim for. If you exceed 100 words when pitching your book then you are not pitching it efficiently. Brevity is good at this juncture. The pitch above is 89 words long, to save you checking.

Think of it like a cover blurb
This is not a synopsis. You do not have to fit everything in. You need to make someone want to read your book in just the same way as publishers use the back-cover blurb. Thankfully, this is really easy to research: just pick up any paperback book and see how it is done. Find some books that are similar in style, scope or potential audience to yours and copy out their blurbs. Actually type them up word for word. You'll find this an excellent way to analyse how it is done, get a feel for the format and tone, and try to replicate that for your pitch.

This is your elevator pitch

It's a clichéd scenario but it works. Imagine you are sharing an elevator ride with an agent/publisher/film producer and you have 30 seconds in which to pitch your story. What can you say to ensure they want to keep the conversation going when the elevator doors open? Stick that down in your pitch.

The synopsis

Writing a synopsis is not easy and requires a different set of skills to writing a novel, or even a pitch. It is one of the most difficult parts of the process and is a common stumbling block with submissions. But don't get in too much of a panic about it. Hardly anyone can write a good synopsis, and agents and publishers know that. This is not an excuse to be sloppy, however, and what follows are some tips to help you create the best synopsis you can.

What a synopsis is NOT

A cover blurb

You've already done the cover blurb thing with your pitch, you don't need to do it again, only longer.

A novella

Neither is this just a cut-down version of your book. It is a summary of it. It needs to be short.

A summary of every plot and sub-plot

In order to write a synopsis you will need to leave a lot of stuff out, and that may well mean dropping sub-plots or sections of the book that are not immediately relevant to the central plot.

Spoiler-free

Please do not worry about revealing the twist, or the ending, or the secret identity. The synopsis needs to contain the whole plot, from start to finish, spoilers and all.

More than 500 words

I have spoken with some agents who feel that anything over 300 words is superfluous but a maximum of 500 is going to be acceptable to pretty much everyone. Any more and you are pushing your luck. Don't say I didn't warn you. However, do remember my mantra of reading the guidelines. Occasionally an agent will request a longer synopsis, in which case you may have more room to play with.

More than a page long

In general, though, if your synopsis is longer than a page in normal font then it is probably too long. I don't care if you think you need an extra paragraph. You are wrong. Again, consider the poor recipient. Do you think they would rather receive a concise, 500-word synopsis that does a great job of summarising the plot, or a four-page one?

What a synopsis IS

A simple summary of the plot

That's all it is. A summary of what happens in the book, leaving out anything that distracts from the central plot. Your pitch can be colourful and emotive and work as a piece of advertising. Your synopsis is cold and direct and functional. Writing it will probably do your head in.

Straightforward

If your synopsis is confusing, then the assumption will be that your book is too. Avoid convoluted backtracking or introducing surprise elements.

Unemotional

All your lyricism and emotion can go into the book itself; there is no room for these things in a synopsis. Strip out any emotive language, any attempts to drive pace or write poetic sentences. Keep it simple. It may seem dull but it needs to do a specific job for you.

The one-sentence synopsis

If you find yourself struggling to write your synopsis, and especially if you are finding it hard to keep it to one page, here's a method that may help, as it forces you to be ruthless to start with and cut things right back to the bare bones before gradually building it back up.

Summarise your book in one sentence

If you absolutely had to explain your book in no more than a single sentence, how would you do it? This will cut through to the very essence of your book, removing any excess baggage.

Expand that to 50 words

Now, add a few more words or sentences to flesh out your summary. 50 words is not a lot, though, so you'll have to be frugal. What you are left with should be a really concise, tight, simple summary of your book.

Now increase to 250 words

OK, now you can elaborate a bit and fill in the gaps. Do everything you can to fit your entire plot into this space.

Do you need more? How successful have you been? If you have done the job then stop right there, you really don't need to go on.

One last go, but keep it under 500. If you absolutely must add some more detail then do so but go over 500 words at your peril.

Sample chapters

As mentioned already, every publisher and agent will have guidelines for what sort of material they want to see and how they want it presented, so I am not going to pre-empt or second-guess that here. What I am going to do is give you a simple checklist that is well worth running through.

You'd be surprised (or maybe not, now that you have read this far) how many authors prepare really strong cover letters, synopses and pitch packages but let themselves down with a poorly-presented sample of work.

Do this stuff, and it shouldn't happen to you:

Follow the guidelines

I know, I know, I have said this before but it bears repeating. What sample content has the agent or publisher asked for? If three chapters, then send them three chapters. If 10,000 words, then send them 10,000 words.

Apart from clear exceptions – your first three chapters are only 50 words in total, your book is only 9,000 words long – you need to do as you are told. And if you are an exception, check with the agent first and see what they want you to do.

Format correctly

Nearly all agents will want you to send your sample chapters as a Microsoft Word document. If you use different word-processing software then you may need to export your work as a Word file. If you are doing that then check that it opens correctly and looks OK on someone else's computer before sending it in as part of the submission.

I tend to read my submissions on my Kindle, and Word documents are far easier to read on that device than PDFs, as the former are more flexible and can be viewed at any font size. Worth bearing in mind if you were thinking of sending in PDF format.

If in doubt, or formatting is not mentioned in the

guidelines, go for Times New Roman as your font and format the document so that the lines are double-spaced.[16]

Check for typos

Agents and publishers aren't too worried by the occasional spelling error, but a manuscript littered with them just seems sloppy and doesn't show your work in the best light. Ideally you would get someone else to read over your work and check for any spelling, grammar or punctuation errors before you send it out. A second pair of eyes can be useful because you may well have become 'blind' to your own errors at this stage, having written and read through all the content several times.

Non-fiction book proposal

If you are submitting a non-fiction title such as a history book, science book or biography, then you may be doing so before the book is completed. This is not unusual for non-fiction, although it is actively discouraged for novels. As always, I will refer you to the agent or publisher guidelines, but if you are a leading expert on Victorian architecture and want to write a book about it then it would be acceptable to pitch the concept to an agent or publisher before going off and doing all the research and writing.

When doing this, you would still be expected to provide

---

16   This refers to the space between each line of text. All word processing software allows you to set the 'spacing' and the default for a submission should be 'double' or '2'.

a query letter containing a pitch but instead of a synopsis you would create a broader proposal, a separate document that explains a bit about the book. There are no hard and fast rules about how this should be formatted but I would suggest it needs to contain the following:

Book summary

A paragraph or two that simply and concisely explains the concept of the book. If it is a history book, talk about which period and subjects it covers. With a biography of a famous person, explain who that person is and what their achievements are. If you have written a science book, outline the key themes and arguments. You get the idea. This is a taster of what the finished book will contain.

Book detail

Having whetted their appetite with the summary, you can go into a bit more detail here. Perhaps 500-1000 words that expand upon the summary and explain the book. It works a bit like a synopsis, but as most non-fiction books do not have a strict plot, as such, you don't need to walk us through the entire 'story' from start to finish. Summarise the book's contents so that the recipient has a clear picture of what you are trying to do.

The market

Although the agent or publisher does not expect you to be a marketing expert, they will consider it a plus if you have an understanding of the potential audience for your book. If you have written that book on Victorian architecture I mentioned above, then some stats about how many other people are interested in the subject would help; a Facebook group with a million members, a monthly magazine with 50,000 subscribers – that sort of thing. Also, some awareness of previous books on similar subjects would be good.

Biography

Time to say a little bit about yourself, but focusing on your qualifications and why you are the person to write this book. If you are the country's leading expert on your subject, make that clear. If you have been given access to rare archives, mention it. And, obviously, details of any previous books you have written would help your case.

Chapter breakdown

As mentioned earlier, many non-fiction books are pitched to, and signed up by, agents and publishers before they are written. In these cases, for obvious reasons, you can't really provide sample chapters so a chapter breakdown is usually expected instead.

Very simply this is a list of your planned chapters, in order, with a few lines of summary for each. At the end of the day, it will take the agent through your concept of the book and give them a clear idea of what you have in mind.

For example:

Introduction
A short introduction outlining the importance of Victorian architecture, how it influenced building design for many years and why a new study is needed.

Chapter One
A brief history of roof tiles and how they were used by 19th-century architects in domestic and commercial buildings.

Chapter Two
A look at the revolution in doorsteps and doorstep-making technology in the 1870s. Includes never-before-seen details of the manufacturing process.

OK, so I am making this nonsense up, but I am sure you get the idea. More than three or four sentences for each summary is probably pushing it.

Although a set of completed chapters is not expected, if you are able to include some sample writing, perhaps just one draft chapter, it would help. An agent might love your proposal and love the sound of your book but simply not engage with your writing, in which case they are not the agent for you. Or, to flip that, they might not be totally convinced by your proposal but love your writing style and that alone may make them want to work with you.

A final non-fiction book submission would ideally include the proposal, chapter breakdown and sample writing as one document – the fewer attachments the better – but, as always, check the guidelines first.

A few words about...

Much of the advice in this book can be applied equally whether you are writing fiction or non-fiction, and the big publishing machine consumes and spews out both in broadly similar ways, but things are different when it comes to poetry and short stories.

Most agents won't represent authors who just write poetry or short stories – for the simple reason that there isn't much money to be made from them. And there are few publishers, outside of specialist presses, who will consider unsolicited submissions from poets and short-story writers. So writers of these forms of writing, and I count myself among them, have to adopt a different strategy.

Traditionally the route to book publication for poets and storywriters starts out with magazines and competitions. You submit your work to a range of online and print publications as well as some of the many competitions that are open to all-comers. Hopefully, over time, you will start to get your work published in some of these mags, or get commendations or even win prizes in competitions. You build up a body of work that has been endorsed and supported by the poetry or story world and you, albeit gradually, start to get your name out there.

This doesn't guarantee you'll ever get a book deal, of course, but the more success you have with mags and prizes the better your chances are, and there are hundreds of opportunities to submit your work – just a quick internet search away..

...poetry and short stories

Follow-up

Did I say writing the synopsis was the most difficult part of the submissions process? I was lying. Waiting for a response is the most difficult part. Now would be a good time to take up a new hobby or redecorate the spare room. Anything to take your mind off the fact that your much-loved creation is now in the hands of someone who could make or break it.

Leave it two months before chasing

If you attempt to chase earlier than this you will just come across as impatient and annoying. Agents and editors have lots of stuff to read. Agents, in particular, spend the bulk of their days reading submissions. It can take some time to get round to yours. Most will respond within a reasonable period but they do not expect you to hang around forever. A polite email asking if they are still interested after two to four months will do the job. If you do not hear back after that then it is fair to move on.

Consider the time of year

The London Book Fair in April and Frankfurt Book Fair in October keep agents extremely busy with lots of preparation and follow-up involved. If you have sent something in March or September then perhaps be prepared to wait a bit longer for a reply. August and January can also be quiet times, with lots of agents buggering off to their gîtes in France or family piles in the Cotswolds.

Take rejection with good grace

Every agent and publisher has horror stories about authors who got nasty/went a bit doolally/turned into an arsehole when receiving a rejection. If you receive a standard stock rejection, just accept it as one of those things that happens and move on. If you receive some feedback, but your book is still rejected, be grateful and take the feedback on board. Do not get back in touch for more clarification, to complain that you have been unfairly treated, to bitch about the agent etc.

Do not re-send unless invited

Even if you have received some helpful feedback it is not the done thing to resubmit the same book to an agent after rejection. If an agent wants you to do some work on your book and then resend it they will make that very clear.

Move on to the next name on your list

When you receive a rejection from one agent, you can then send your book to another. If you are working in groups of five or six then select the next in line, repeat the whole research process for them and then send your work.

Success

Let's be optimistic for a moment. Let's forget the odds that are stacked against you, and the rejection emails sitting in your inbox, and assume that an agent likes your submission and wants to read more. What happens next?

Well, first up, of course, you need to have something else to give them to read, especially in the case of fiction. I know of some cases where a writer has managed to get over the first hurdle, have their full manuscript called in, only to confess that the rest of the novel isn't quite ready, or isn't even finished. I am sure there are things that would piss off an agent more than this, but there won't be many.

You will almost certainly be asked to send in the full manuscript. If the agent, or publisher, has any specific guidelines they will make them clear in their request. By now you should know how I feel about guidelines. Just follow them. If there are no guidelines offered then don't bother the agent with lots of follow-up questions, just make sure the manuscript is formatted in the same style as your submission and get ready to send it.

With non-fiction, the next steps will depend on the status of the manuscript. If the manuscript is complete then all of the above remains relevant.

If your non-fiction book is incomplete, and you made that clear in your submission, then the agent is almost certainly going to be more specific in their request. Pay attention to what they ask for. They may want more sample material, or a more detailed chapter breakdown, or they might want to chat about the book over the phone or in person. As always, it pays to simply do as they ask and not overcomplicate things.

Having spent so much time perfecting your submission it makes sense to spend some time checking over your manuscript before sending it off. Now is not the time to rewrite big chunks of it, even if you are suddenly experiencing a crisis of confidence, but it would be good to read through the whole thing once more to mop up any typos or fix any little glitches. It doesn't have to be absolutely perfect but let's make it as good as possible before sending it off.

Once you send it off then yet another waiting game begins.

If an agent has called in your manuscript then the chances are they will be reading it themselves and, given all the other stuff they are working on, this will take time. How long does it take you to read a book? A couple of days? A week? Two? Well, an agent could well take that long, or even more, to finish reading yours. We hope, of course, that they drop everything as soon as your manuscript arrives, and that might happen, but let's be realistic.

When the response does come, it could take one of several forms.

Rejection

The agent may decide, having read the whole book, that it is not for them. This does not mean that the book isn't publishable and that all your hopes are dashed, just that this particular agent didn't feel they could add anything to the package, or find the right home, or didn't quite love it enough to want to represent it. You would hope that a rejection at this stage will include some specific feedback but that won't always happen. If it does, embrace it and digest it, it should be very useful as you dust yourself off and go back out there with your book.

Rewrite

The agent may get back to you with suggestions or requests for rewrites. This is a very good sign, as it means they are clearly interested in the book, but it does not constitute an offer. Many authors have rewritten their entire books, sometimes a number of times, only for an agent to ultimately decide not to take it on, but we are being optimistic for a while, so let's move on.

Meeting

Most agents will want to meet an author before offering to represent them. This is a process that has benefits for both parties. The agent will be your professional partner in your writing career and it is important that the two of you click. You don't have to be best mates (although that does happen sometimes) but you do need to get on and respect each other.

Of course, a meeting isn't always possible but a phone call, or Skype session, is a reasonable alternative. Either way, you need to have a good natter about you, your work and the plans you both have for it.

At this stage, the relationship takes an interesting turn. Having spent the last several weeks and months trying to convince an agent to take on your work, you now have an agent trying to convince you to employ them to represent you. Don't let all the power go to your head but, you know, allow yourself a little smile.

I won't linger any more on this; this is a chapter about perfecting your submission and we are in danger of moving all the way to publication, which is something I cover in a forthcoming chapter.

Some positive thoughts

I realise I have spent the last several pages saying 'Do this' and 'Don't do that' and generally telling you how hard this whole process would be, so, just before we come to the end of this chapter, I want to share some positive thoughts.

Every time an agent or publisher opens up a submission, they want it to be amazing. They want it to be something they fall in love with, that they cannot put down. They want to get to the end of the sample chapters with an urge to read more. They really do want you to succeed. And therefore they'll be quite forgiving.

We do not expect your submission to be perfect. We'll overlook little errors and issues, especially if your story is strong and compelling. We are, in the main, quite nice people. Honest.

But we do get sent a lot of things to read, a lot of things to consider, and over the years we have developed certain skills, certain shorthand, for identifying manuscripts that are, in all probability, not for us. I just don't want you to fall foul of any of that.

Also, don't view every rejection as a negative thing. You deserve to be represented or published by someone who loves your work. If someone reads your submission and is lukewarm about it, it is probably a good thing that they don't sign you up – you want someone to champion your writing, to shout about how great you are – and you definitely don't want to be involved with someone who doesn't like your work at all and is only in it for the money. The submissions process is about finding someone who is right for you and your book; it is unlikely to happen immediately.

Just remember, we really do want your book to be wonderful. There is nothing we like more.

Conclusion

So there you have it, my advice on how to perfect your submission. I cannot guarantee you will get your book published – it could be terrible for all I know – but, if you follow these guidelines, you will have avoided the mistakes that other aspiring writers make on a regular basis, you will have pulled together a strong submission package and you will have given yourself, and your work, the best chance to take the next steps towards publication.

If you do get published, what lies ahead of you is every bit as scary, daunting and unpredictable as the submissions process has been. You and your work will be pulled apart, scrutinised, criticised and reviewed, and sometimes that won't be a very pleasant experience, but if your book ends up in the hands of one reader, just one reader, for whom it really means something, then it will have all been worth it.

Good luck. You're going to need it.

15

Self-publishing

Little more than a decade ago self-publishing was seen as either the last resort for authors who were not 'good enough' to find a traditional publisher, or a simple act of vanity. In fact, it was known for many years as vanity publishing, but all that has changed and publishing your own book is now not only a viable option for most authors, but also one that can be considerably more lucrative than the traditional route.

The advent of ebooks and advancements in digital printing have revolutionised the self-publishing market and proved to publishers and agents that they don't have a monopoly on popular books. Some of the bestselling books of recent years – *Fifty Shades of Grey*, *The Martian*, *Killing Eve*, to name just a few – were originally self-published and have made their authors shedloads of money. What's more, choosing to self-publish doesn't close the door on traditional publishing; the three books I just mentioned all went on to be successful when re-issued by large publishers.

But self-publishing can be bloody hard work and take up a lot of your time if you plan to do it properly. What follows is a short guide to the pros and cons of the process.

You are no longer a writer

As the name suggests, when you self-publish you become your own publisher, so you are no longer just a writer. If you decide to do everything yourself (which I strongly urge you not to do) then you become developmental editor, copyeditor, proofreader, typographer, cover designer, publicist, marketer, sales person, returns co-ordinator and financial manager. These are all roles that require different skills, can take considerable time, and often need to be handled simultaneously.

Set a budget

Although it is technically possible to self-publish an ebook without spending any money, most people will pay one or more professionals to do some of the work for them. Calculate how much you can afford to spend on editing, design and marketing. When doing this, assume you won't make any of it back, as there is no guarantee that you will.

How much can you comfortably afford to lose on this project? I don't mean this in a negative way – we all spend money on hobbies and activities without ever expecting to make a profit – just being realistic. Work out how much you want to spend and then allocate the money to the key tasks, which would usually be cover design and editing, but may also including typesetting and printing.

Get an editor

I am not just saying this because it is how I make most of my living but, for the love of all that is holy, please get your book professionally edited. Even I, a professional editor, got another editor to go through the book I self-published. No matter how confident you are that your book is close to perfect, an editor will find grammatical errors and typos, plot inconsistencies, areas that could be improved or even things that just don't make sense. One of the reasons that self-published books have had a bad reputation, especially those published on Amazon and other digital platforms, is because many have not been edited – and it shows, it really shows.

Hiring an editor need not cost the earth, but it will cost you something. I recommend checking out the Reedsy website[17] where you can put out a request and outline your budget, and prospective editors can come back with quotes. You can hire someone to give you a detailed structural edit,

---

17   More on Reedsy in the Resources section towards the end of the book.

an editorial assessment, a copyedit to sort any errors, or just a proofread. If your book is 100,000 words long then you could expect to pay between £1,500-£2000 for a big, all bells-and-whistles structural edit. An editorial assessment or copyedit could be £500-£1000, and a proofread closer to £500. That would be to employ industry professionals to do the job for you. You can absolutely get the work cheaper, and you may find someone on Reedsy prepared to do it for less, but I wanted to give you an idea of the sort of costs you'd be looking at.

Don't put a shitty cover on it

If self-published books have a bad rep when it comes to editing, they have a disastrous one when it comes to covers. So many self-published books have covers that would never be allowed anywhere near the shelves of a bookshop. They look amateurish, and while they say you can't tell a book by its cover, you can certainly decide not to buy a book that has an awful cover. I talk about this in more detail on the following pages but do yourself a favour and get a professional to design your book cover. It should cost you £100-200 for an ebook cover and £400-500 for a full print cover.

A few words about...

A book cover is trying to do several things at once.
It is attempting to convey, in an instant, the kind of
book it is. With most books you should be able tell,
without reading any of the words on the front, if it is a
crime novel or a romance, for example. It does this with
various visual clues, some of which, such as an image of a
woman running down a darkened street in crime fiction,
have become quite clichéd – but they do help the reader
identify whether or not a book is for them. The type of
font, colours used and layout can all be indicators of genre
or style or expected readership.

This book, for example, has an image of a typewriter on
the front and the title is big and bold. It should be pretty
obvious from a distance that this is not a hilarious rom-
com.

Once it has got your attention it then tries to convince
you to invest some time checking it out. This is achieved
through a combination of endorsements (quotes from
other authors or newspaper and magazine reviews) and
a strapline or subtitle (a short, pithy phrase that tries to
explain the book or entice you in).

Again, looking at the book you have in your hands
now, we have a subtitle – *A Guide to Writing, Editing,
Submitting and Publishing Your Book* – that makes it clear
what the book is about. I chose a punchy quote – 'Shut

up and listen to everything he has to say' – to put on the front because it is an excellent call to action and also hints that the book does not take itself too seriously.

Then we have the cover copy, the blurb that sits on the back of the book, or inside flap if it is a hardback. This is usually 100-200 words that act as part-summary, part-advertising spiel and are intended to reaffirm that this really is the book for you.

With *Tips from a Publisher* we went for a short blurb explaining the book, a brief bio of me and some more quotes all saying nice things about me or the book. I wouldn't normally put a bio on the cover but it seemed like a good thing to do with this book as most readers won't have a clue who I am.

If you are being published traditionally then pretty much all of the above will be looked after for you and my advice is not to worry too much about the minutiae – the hair colour isn't quite right, I didn't imagine that sort of building, I don't like red – as long as the end result is striking and appealing.

If you are self-publishing, it is important that you consider these basic functions of a cover and try to create something that could sit alongside the bestsellers in your genre.

...book covers

Your book probably won't sell

It is hard enough for an established publisher to sell more than a thousand or so copies of a book without a fair bit of marketing spend, good reviews, bookshop support and a lot of luck. It is way harder for a self-published author to make their book visible, let alone sell it. The vast majority of self-published books, perhaps 95% of them, will sell just a handful of copies and those will be to friends and relatives. Don't get your hopes up. Sorry to piss on your picnic like that.

The value of free

If you are publishing a series of books, a trilogy or longer sequence, then you may want to consider making the first book available for free. Lots of people who read ebooks scout the free book charts on Amazon and elsewhere and load up their devices. OK, a lot of these do not get read but many of them do and if someone reads and enjoys your free book they are more likely to post a review and, importantly, much more likely to read the next book in the series which, of course, you charge them for. Lure them in with a freebie and some will stay and pay for more.

Do you need a print edition?

I generally advise self-published authors to start out by just publishing an ebook. No need to go to the additional cost involved in a print edition – typesetting, full cover, ISBN, printing, warehousing and distribution – until you know if there is a market. If you can sell several thousand ebooks then there is a reasonable indication that you could sell a print edition too, but don't print books until you know if you can sell them.

Sure, if your local bookshop has promised to stock it and you have a social network that you know will buy copies, or if you are a public speaker able to flog books at your events, then it might be worth considering, but most bookshops won't go near self-published books and there aren't that many places to sell them in any quantity.

Start small

When I have self-published books I started out by publishing them purely as ebooks on Amazon, using their KDP platform. It was easy to use and I was able to upload a Word document for the text and a jpeg for the cover and get everything sorted and in place. I created the ebook and pressed the button to send it off. I then had to wait a day or so until Amazon confirmed it was live on their site. And then I paid to download it so that I could experience what a reader would if they bought my ebook.

But I didn't tell anyone else about it.

I wanted to test the system, see how it all worked, and give myself the opportunity to make mistakes. I spotted some typos I had missed, some layout niggles that were not clear until I read the book on my Kindle, and noticed something I could do to make the cover a bit better. I was also able to read and revise the text that appears on the book's main page on Amazon. Essentially I tested everything and refined it before I took the next step.

Once I was happy I uploaded the book to other sales platforms and started to spread the word, but I am glad I started small and quietly and was able to fix all my mistakes before anyone else got to see it.

Where to publish

If you are publishing purely digitally then the obvious place to start is Amazon. In the UK they have close to 90% of the ebook market (even though they won't admit it) and although they are less dominant in the US they are the biggest ebook retailer on the planet by a long chalk. So, if you want to sell ebooks you do really need to make yours available on their site, even if you don't like the fact that they pay next to fuck-all tax, don't let their factory workers use the toilets when they need to (allegedly) and their founder is spaffing away his billions on space travel when he could eradicate much of world poverty and still have cash left over for a few over-compensatory rockets. If you want your ebook to reach the widest possible audience then you might just need to bury your moral compass for a short while and be a bit selfish.

The Amazon KDP platform is pretty easy to use and allows anyone to self-publish an ebook as long as they have a Word document and a jpeg for the cover. It takes 15 minutes or so to fill out the online form, upload the files and set up your Amazon listing for your book. And it will be available worldwide a day or so after you press the button.

Kobo and Barnes & Noble also have fairly easy platforms for self-publishing and once you have mastered Amazon these will be a piece of piss. Apple, on the other hand, is a massive pain in the arse, and to be honest, I got so pissed off with their upload system that I just gave up. In the UK they have just 1 or 2% of the market so I am not really losing out on sales.

If you can't be arsed to upload to several different sites, or if you just get annoyed at Apple's ridiculous system like I did, then there are a number of companies that can look after all that stuff for you. Websites such as Smashwords, INscribe Digital, BookBaby and Draft2Digital are effectively ebook aggregators that allow you to upload just once and they check your files and distribute across all retail platforms, including subscription services such as Scribd and 24Symbols. I found Draft2Digital pretty easy to use but you should check out a range of options before deciding what is best for you.

Marketing

I had never heard the word 'discoverability' until a decade or so ago. I am not even sure it is a real word. Anyway, when used in a publishing context, and especially relevant when it comes to self-publishing, it translates as 'how will people find your book?' With hundreds of thousands of books published every year by established publishers, and many times that by self-published authors, how on earth will anyone notice that yours exists?

As a self-published author you will need to fight hard and shout loud in order to get any sort of profile for yourself or your work, and that is especially hard to do while avoiding spamming or annoying people. Thankfully it happens a lot less now, but there was a period in the early days of Amazon's self-publishing renaissance when I would receive unsolicited tweets, Facebook messages and even emails from authors plugging their books. Spam, in other words. I am not sure this ever worked. It certainly didn't with me.

So you do need to think about how to spread the word about your book. You can get a marketing company or freelance publicity person to help you out but these will cost money. Ask them for examples of other projects they have worked on and see if you think their track record is strong enough.

You can also employ someone to arrange a blog tour for you. This is where a series of bloggers 'host' you or your book on their site and post a review or interview or feature to help spread the word about your book. These are usually lined up one after another across a week or so and can be quite effective, especially for genre fiction.

Check out my 'A Few Words About…' section on social media for more thoughts about marketing and publicity in the digital age.

You won't have much time to write

The number-one complaint I hear from my self-published author friends is that they don't have enough time to write. They find a lot of time is eaten up with other tasks related to self-publishing, and sitting down to write the next book keeps getting pushed back, or has to be squeezed into a short period of time each week.

This chapter is intended to offer some tips, and get you thinking about the issues you may face and ensure you don't launch yourself into the world of self-publishing without first doing a lot of research. You need to be sure that it is the right route for you and your book. You also need to plan ahead and budget sensibly.

16

Life as an Author

Most of this book, for obvious reasons, has focused on various steps and strategies to help you in your mission to become a published author. Along the way I have tried to open up the publishing world to you, sharing trade secrets and the sort of stuff that authors are rarely told about. As we near the end of the book, I also want to explore, albeit briefly, what happens once you are a published author.

We have already looked at some aspects of this. In the 'Life-cycle of a Book' chapter you have seen what happens to your manuscript once a publisher gets hold of it, and in the recent chapter on submissions there was a section covering what happens immediately after an agent signs you up. In this chapter I want to share with you what other writers have experienced post-publication. I asked authors I know well to answer a simple question for me: *What do you wish you had known before you were a published author?*

I have gone through their answers and picked out the most common themes and responses, to make sure you know what they didn't.

Getting published is just part of the journey, not the destination

Authors focus so much on getting published that they can understandably view it as the end goal. Mission accomplished. In reality, you are only part-way there. It could even be viewed as a new beginning. There is so much more ahead of you than behind you – editing, production, marketing, publicity, publication, reviews, book events – and you are not in control of any of them.

Manage your expectations

Because so much of what lies ahead is managed by other people, sometimes the only thing you can manage are your own expectations. There will be disappointments ahead. Your book might not be stocked by your favourite bookshop, you might not get asked to do any book events, there may be no press reviews, or you do get reviews but they are not good ones. Hopefully the good stuff will far outweigh the bad, but you do need to be prepared for the fact that things won't always run smoothly.

Don't give up the day job

Unless your book becomes a massive bestseller, or you are an author who writes a book every year and those books sell pretty well, you are highly unlikely to earn enough money to live off comfortably. Most published authors have other jobs. I have published and edited authors with careers as varied as nurse, rock musician, postman, football manager, teacher, stand-up comedian, lawyer, bookseller, doctor, classical music conductor and social worker. Some are full-time writers, but most are not, and that is true of the industry as a whole.

You'll have to do a fair bit yourself

One consistent message from the authors I surveyed was that, after an initial period of publicity around publication, publishers tend to move on to other books and other authors fairly quickly. If you remember my conveyor belt analogy from the 'Life-cycle of a Book' chapter (and how could you forget it?) publicists in particular only work on books for a few weeks before they have to stop and focus on the next one. As a result many authors resort to doing their own publicity once their book is a few months old. This may be purely on social media or by contacting bloggers and reviewers, organising their own book events or pitching articles related to their book to newspapers and magazines. Some more established authors even employ their own year-round publicists, but that can be costly. Essentially, don't expect your publisher to be promoting your book six months after publication.

Be a good networker

Tell people about your work, whether that be in person or online, but don't be some sort of spam machine. Share your excitement and experiences and you will find that many people are on your side and want you to be a success. But be supportive of others, too. Offer advice and help to other authors, bloggers, readers. Be your book's biggest cheerleader and your enthusiasm may well prove to be infectious.

A few words about...

At several points during your life as an author you will be required to sign a contract. It may be when appointing an agent, or finalising a publishing deal, or selling film rights for millions of dollars. Whenever it happens it would be prudent to get legal advice from a professional but, just as a heads-up, here are the key things to look out for. Even if you are somewhat blinded by the peculiar legalese of the language used in contracts it is important that you understand these elements of a book contract.

Rights. When you sign a contract relating to your writing you are usually giving someone else the *right* to do something with your work. Make sure you are aware of what these rights are and how long they last for. Typically, in a book contract, the publisher will have the right to produce print and digital editions in an agreed territory for the length of copyright but they may also include audiobook, film, television and merchandise rights. Make sure you know what you are signing up for.

Obligations. What are you, and the other party, obliged to do as part of the contract? As an author you would usually expect to be given a deadline for delivery of your book and a target word-count at the very least. The publisher would be expected to commit to a rough publication date.

Payment. The amount of your advance and the royalty rates for sales, and any other income, should be made clear. Likewise, payment dates.

Termination. It is important that there is a clear and understandable get-out clause in the contract. Often this would be linked to sales, so if a book goes out of print or sales fall below a certain level then the author can ask for the contract to be terminated.

Different business models and different types of arrangement may require different forms of contract but, broadly speaking, you will always want to know what rights are involved and for how long, what is expected of you, how you'll get paid and what you need to do to get out of the whole thing if required. And with all of these elements, if you aren't sure what you are signing up to then you are well within your rights to ask and also to request that the wording is made clearer in the document itself.

In the UK, members of the Society of Authors can have any contract checked and vetted by one of their legal team – a service well worth using.

...**contracts**

You won't know how your book is selling

Publishers rarely share precise details of book sales with their authors outside of royalty statements. I like to, and will always give up-to-date information to my authors when asked, but I am in the minority. Your editor may give you a general idea, perhaps, but most are very cautious. They have good reason. Because our industry operates on a sale-or-return basis, a publisher could send out 25,000 copies of a book and get 20,000 back, so they don't want to get an author's hopes up. But there is also a tradition of keeping authors in the dark when it comes to this stuff. I don't think that is on, quite frankly, but it is still the norm.

Lots of people won't like your book

Your significant other loves your book. Your agent loves your book. Your editor loves your book. Between acceptance and publication everyone is saying great things about you and your work, but this will not last. Once your book is out there and real people start to read it, they will tell you what they think. Newspaper reviewers, readers who post an Amazon rating, someone on GoodReads, tweeters, Instagrammers –

all manner of people will have an opinion. And here's the thing: their opinion is correct. If they don't like it, they don't like it, and if they want to tell other people, then that is their prerogative. No book receives unanimously positive reviews and yours will be no exception.

And that is fine. I tell my authors that they haven't truly arrived on the literary scene until they have received their first stinker of a review. It may not be nice, and sometimes it will really sting, but it will happen. Find a way to deal with it.

Be nice

Publishing is incestuous. Not literally, at least not as far as I know, but people move from job to job, from publisher to publisher with some frequency. Today's bookseller is tomorrow's publisher, the publicist who worked on your first book might be the editor of your fourth, an editorial assistant may end up being a CEO further down your career. Be nice to the people who work with you on your book as a) that is the decent thing to do and b) you never know what they might be doing next or how much they can help you in the future.

Everyone in the book world knows who the nice authors are and they also know which authors are arseholes. We can all name them. For example, you won't find anyone in publishing with a bad word to say about Ali Smith, David Mitchell or Sarah Waters, who are always considerate, appreciative, and friendly with everyone they come across.

In response to this, booksellers, publicists and journalists go out of their way to be supportive. And while I can't list the arseholes for legal reasons, I know that the efforts made on their behalf tend to be less fulsome, less willing.

It helps if you love writing

Ultimately, if you love writing and telling stories then you always have that to fall back on. No matter how good or bad your publishing experience is, if at the heart of it is a process you love then that will fuel and power your creative life.

Editing can be a pain in the arse

So many authors love the writing process but hate the editing process. Not all, but many. Be prepared for a lot of wrangling with your text to get things right.

You are not alone

You are entering what is largely a supportive world of fellow writers, publishers, bloggers, and readers. It is a true community, especially online, and they can help you navigate the difficult parts of the job.

Be prepared to fail

Not everything you do will be a success. You will sometimes fail, and you may fail spectacularly. That is perfectly OK, as long as you learn from your failures.

Don't take anything for granted

Appreciate the moment. Don't assume things will always be the same. If you are enjoying success today, it may not remain at that level. Likewise, if your current book doesn't sell well, your next one might be your breakthrough. Publishing is mercurial and we often don't know why some books work and others fail.

You need to write something else now

The editing and production process, the excitement around publication, book signings, reviews and interviews, festival appearances are all wonderful things that, if we are honest, get in the way of writing your next book. For many authors, publication of their debut book comes slap-bang in the middle of writing the follow-up. Be prepared for interruptions. They are good interruptions but they are interruptions nonetheless.

It will be OK

There will be bumps in the road and setbacks. There will be good days and bad days. There may well be tears. But it will be OK in the end. You are a published author, and that is a wonderful achievement that no one can take away from you.

In summary: success may be fleeting but the same can be said for failure; publication may be the end of one journey but it is the start of an even longer one; you may have to do a lot of work yourself; brace yourself for bad reviews; join the welcoming and supportive community of writers and readers; and, most importantly of all, be nice.

However, bear in mind that you are part of a unique creative industry. At any moment of any day, someone could walk into a bookshop, or open up a webpage, and buy your book. Having done so, they could read it and love it; it could even change their lives. However big your audience, if it is an appreciative one then there are few achievements greater than that for an author.

Which is what you are now: an author. Congratulations.

Extras

17

FAQs

I hope I have covered much of what you need to know in this book, but here are some questions that I, and other publishers and agents, get asked a lot.

The publishing world

Q: Can I make a living as an author?
A: From books alone, probably not. Unless your work is regularly in the bestseller charts it would be hard to deliver what most people would consider a decent salary. From the wider world of books and writing, perhaps. I write books, edit books, give classes and workshops, teach on a university-degree course, write quiz questions for TV shows, and pen

the occasional article – all of which comes under a broad books and writing umbrella – and make a modest living out of it. Other authors I know focus more on journalism and create revenue that way. Many are full- or part-time teachers in publishing or creative writing. You can certainly earn a reasonable amount from your books if they sell well but most authors have other sources of income as well.

Q: How much input does an author get into how their book is published?

A: It differs from publisher to publisher. Most do try to keep the author informed on how things are going during production and will often consult them on key decisions but at the end of the day they are investing thousands of pounds into the project and will almost always default to what they consider to be the most commercial option when it comes to the finished product. If you are offered some input on cover and text design then that is great but it is not guaranteed. You are highly unlikely to be consulted on things such as publication date, format or price. My advice is that it is fine for you to ask questions about this stuff but when an author starts meddling too much, or making lots of demands, it can be detrimental to the working relationship.

Q: What if I don't like a decision my publisher has made?

A: Communication is key in any relationship so I would always recommend informing your publisher when you are uncomfortable with something. If you have an agent then this can come though them, and that removes you from any direct confrontation should things escalate. I would hope that a decent publisher would listen to your concerns but also explain why they have made a particular decision. Ultimately, it is their call, and you need to respect that, but this is your book and your writing career so don't feel you can't speak up.

Q: An agent is interested in my work but is insisting I make a change to my manuscript that I am really unhappy with. Am I right to stick to my guns?

A: That depends on how much you want to work with this agent. I won't pretend that agents are always correct but it is a fair bet that they know the book world better than you do, and if they feel they have a better chance of selling your book if you make changes then you really need to consider them. Of course, feel free to stick to your guns but doing so might lose you this chance of publication and there is no guarantee another will come.

Q: How do I find out how many copies of my book have sold?

A: The easy answer is to ask your publisher but, to be honest, publishers are not great when it comes to sharing sales information. You will receive a six-monthly royalty statement which will contain details of your sales but any details outside of that will be down to how communicative your publisher wants to be. I am always prepared to share this information with my authors, even if it isn't good news, but publishers are busy people and often have lots of authors to look after so can't spend too much time checking and sharing sales data.

Q: I have been offered a deal by a publisher but I don't have an agent. I am a bit lost when it comes to checking the contract they have sent me. What can I do?

A: One excellent option is to join the Society of Authors. I talk about them in more detail in the 'Resources' chapter but one service they offer is contract vetting. They will check though an author's contract and offer feedback on it, including suggestions for changes and other recommendations. Much cheaper than paying a solicitor to look at it and they offer lots of other services too.

Q: If so few books make any money and most authors struggle to make a living, why does anyone bother? Doesn't the industry need to look at what it is doing?

A: An excellent question. I couldn't have put it better myself. Most publishers rely on a relatively small number of books selling so well that they fund the rest *and* help the overall business make a profit. The problem is, there is often no way of knowing which books will work and which won't. Sure, they can be confident that the new Lee Child or Jacqueline Wilson books will sell bucket-loads but they need to publish lots of authors, and lots of books that don't sell, in order to find the new ones that do. It is a very hit-and-miss affair. However, it works just about enough for the model to be sustainable and the industry is too set in its ways to create major upheaval and change things.

A few words about...

A question I am often asked at my talks and workshops is: 'How can I stop people from stealing my work?'

If you have been reading this book from cover to cover then you may already have all the information you need to dismiss this question, but for the dippers-in here are the reasons you don't need to worry about this.

Although you cannot copyright an idea – anyone can write a book about a boy going to wizarding school – the expression of an idea, especially when written down, is automatically copyrighted without you having to do a thing. The moment you write something you own the copyright for it. You don't need to register this anywhere, or pay someone to do that for you. Just by writing it down, you have legal rights to it. Which is why JK Rowling, or more accurately her lawyers, will be in touch with you if your young wizard bears too close a resemblance to Harry Potter.

The chances of someone wanting to steal your work and put their name to it for profit are so slim as to be practically non-existent. It is bloody hard to make money out of any book, let alone trying to do so with an unknown manuscript by an unknown writer. It just isn't going to happen.

And there is absolutely zero-chance of it happening if you follow my advice and only send your work to reputable agents and publishers. These people won't steal your work.

...copyright

Writing

Q: I have read lots of conflicting advice on key aspects of writing. How do I know which advice to follow?

A: In the world of books and writing, so much is subjective. Millions of people love the novels of Dan Brown, and he is a multi-millionaire to prove it, but the majority of professional critics consider him to be, how can I put this, not a great writer. Who is correct? When it comes to opinions, everyone feels they are right. When it comes to processing and implementing advice, I would suggest you absorb the stuff that feels right to you, that resonates. If you read that you should always show and never tell, but the books you love feature a combination of both styles, then don't feel bad if you ignore that advice. If you come across a tip that makes sense to you, and that you know you can apply to your writing, then embrace it.

Submissions

Q: I have previously self-published my work. Will it count against me?

A: This may have been the case a few years ago but there have been so many self-published successes of late that very few agents will be bothered by a self-publishing past. It may even be seen as a bonus, especially if you managed to sell a lot of copies.

In general, agents won't consider taking on books that you have already self-published, unless they have sold bucket-loads, so best not to submit something that has such a background unless the agent has specifically said it is OK.

Suffice to say, any agent who would be bothered by a self-published author isn't the agent for you.

Q: I cannot possibly get my synopsis on one page. Can I submit a two- or three-page synopsis instead?
A: First, you are not trying hard enough. Any book can by summarised in one page if you really focus. But, for the sake of argument, let's assume it is completely impossible to keep the synopsis to just the one page.

If the guidelines for your chosen agent or publisher have a word-count or page-length requirement, and you are currently over that limit – tough luck. Ignore those guidelines at your peril.

If – and some do – your chosen recipient does not have such guidelines then you can, by all means, give it a go. But I have yet to meet an agent or publisher whose heart doesn't sink when they see a three-page synopsis. Why put them through that?

Q: I am not sure what genre to classify my book as. What should I do?
A: Ask yourself this question: In which section of a bookshop do I want my book to be shelved? That's your genre. If you need to be more specific than just 'Fiction' then you could check out the Amazon category for books you feel are similar

to yours and use that. Don't get too specific. 'Fantasy Fiction' is fine, 'Historical Cyberpunk Romance' isn't a genre that many agents will be able to relate to.

Q: Should I outline the market for my novel in my query letter?

A: Authors often do this, and there isn't any harm in it if the information is presented well, but if the agent or publisher hasn't asked for it then it isn't essential. Chances are the agent or publisher will know more about the market than you do anyway. Generally it is not considered a requirement for fiction, but is encouraged for non-fiction.

Q: In my cover letter should I mention any workshops or creative writing classes I have attended?

A: That depends. If you are the graduate of a recognised creative-writing degree course, or a well-known class or workshop, then by all means mention it. The same goes for awards. But little-known or obscure courses aren't really going to help your case all that much. They certainly won't make or break your submission.

Q: Do I need a brand and how much will it hamper me if I haven't got one?

A: I do get asked this a lot. If you have a strong brand, either as the owner of a website or a specialist in a certain field, then it is worth shouting about, and can be particularly useful for non-fiction projects, but it is by no means essential. It can help but the lack of one won't hurt you.

Q: If my work is experimental, plays with genre tropes or otherwise proves unexpected or even controversial, should I warn in advance of let them find out for themselves?

A: If you have followed the guidelines in the submissions chapter correctly then you should know not to hide anything from the agent or publisher. Tell them what they are getting, plain and simple.

Q: Is it OK to resubmit a manuscript to an agent once I have reworked it?

A: Unless you have been requested to resubmit it, then no.

Q: I have received a rejection but I have some follow-up questions. Is it OK to drop the agent an e-mail?

A: No. If the agents wants you to get in touch again they will invite you to do so.

Q: I feel I have been unfairly treated. How do I go about complaining?

A: Grow up. If you receive a rejection, take it with good grace and move on.

Q: I am worried about sending my work out to an agent in case they steal my idea. How can I protect myself against this?

A: Relax. If you are sending your work to a reputable agent or publisher then this really is not going to happen. The chances that your work is so amazing, so incredible, that a publishing professional is going to risk their careers by nicking it are zero. Simply by writing the work in the first place you have automatic copyright, and this is solid protection.

Q: My book has a major plot twist at the end and I don't want to reveal this in the synopsis. Is it OK to keep it secret?

A: No, it isn't. Bear in mind that you are probably only sending a synopsis and a few chapters, so the recipient will have no idea what your twist is, even if they read all the material you have sent, unless you spell it out. If your twist is so bloody great then tell us about it.

Q: I have found an agent who wants to read my work, but they charge a small administration fee. Should I pay it?

A: This one is easy. Never pay anyone a fee when submitting your work. These are always scams. No reputable agent or publisher will charge you anything to read your submission.

Q: Should I pay an editor to work on my manuscript before I submit it?

A: That is up to you. If you have had quality feedback from early readers and are confident that your book is as good as it can be, then you might as well submit it. However, if you have some nagging doubts about certain aspects – plot, character, dialogue or something else – then it may well help to have a publishing professional look over it. It is unlikely that you'll need a line-by-line edit, just an editorial assessment should be enough. This is where an editor reads your book and writes a report on issues, areas of concern, and things that could be improved. It is a service I provide in my day job as a freelance editor, and I work on many such assessments every year.

Q: I have an excellent cover design for my book already. Is it OK to include this with my submission? I want the agent to have an idea of how I want the book to look.
Are you a professional cover designer? I am guessing not. In which case, do not send a cover design. It is never a good idea and can put out the wrong signals. Whenever an author has done this to me the cover has been crap, 100% of the time.

Self-publishing

Q: I cannot afford to pay someone to edit my book or design a cover. Does it really matter?
A: I am not asking you to go into debt to fund your book, and I am well aware that the cost of using professionals will be prohibitive for many writers, but you do need to be aware of the drawbacks if you do not. If you wanted to landscape your garden would you do it all yourself, or hire some help? If you were planning a wedding would you get someone to do the catering, or prepare the flowers, or take the photographs? You could answer *no* to all of those questions and you *might* end up doing a decent job yourself, but would it be as good as the professional version? You

want your book to be primed for success and it is highly unlikely that you have the skills to ensure that every element is as professional as possible.

Q: How can I get my self-published book into bookshops?

A: You probably can't. If you consider the sheer number of self-published authors and their books, it would be impossible for bookshops to stock even a small percentage of them. It just isn't viable, especially as each author would need a trading account with the bookshop and that takes time and resources to set up.

One possible route in is to approach your local bookshop, especially an independent one. They won't always be interested but many do support self-published authors, especially if you can guarantee that your friends and acquaintances will be in to buy copies.

18

Resources

I have listed here all manner of websites, tools, books and other resources that you might find useful while researching, writing, editing, submitting or publishing your book. Personally, I don't like seeing long web addresses in printed books; you can't copy and paste them and they are a pain in the arse to type out. Also, they aren't needed, as a simple web search will help you find them. Instead I have included keywords that you can enter into Google, or whatever search engine you use, to find the right site or page.

Dictionaries

I tend to use the Oxford English Dictionary (**Search: OED**) for most of my research and word checking, and it is particularly helpful when it comes to word origins and history but it is not free to all. You can, however, log in and use it for nothing if you have a UK library card. An excellent free alternative is the Collins Dictionary website (**Search: Collins Dictionary**) which has a splendid feature that shows the frequency of word use over time. So if you need to check to see if the word 'bollocks' would be historically accurate in your novel set in the 18th century[18] then this is a good place to go. UK authors needing to check American spellings and usage should check out the Merriam-Webster online dictionary (**Search: Merriam Webster**) and, obviously, you can flip all this advice if you are in America.

Sound and vision

If you have read this book all the way through then you will have noticed that I go on a fair bit about the need to capture all the senses in your writing if at all possible. What characters hear can be as important, sometimes, as what they see, but researching what a character in another country or another time might be listening to is not always easy. Over

---

18   Spoiler: It would be, but only just.

the years I have come across a few online tools that can help.

Nature SoundMap is a wonderful website that allows you to travel the world and play clips of the sounds of nature from many different locations. So you could listen to dusk by a frog pond in West Papua or birds gathering in the Great Rann of Kutch, the cry of the horned screamer in Peru or grazing bison in Oklahoma, from pigeons in a Surrey garden to an albatross on Midway Atoll. There are hundreds of soundscapes to choose from and they can be of great use to writers who want to track down a specific wildlife sound or are looking to capture the aural landscape of a particular location. I often use it just for background noise while writing and it can be very soothing. (**Search: Nature Sound Map**)

Offering a similar service but much more location specific is the London Sound Survey which has collected dozens of recordings of contemporary London if you need to add a bit of authenticity to your London scenes. But it has lots more too, including historical soundscapes dating back to the 1920s, recordings of waterways, wildlife and even the calls of market traders. (**Search: London Sound Survey**)

Working out what music people might have been listening to at certain points in history can also be helpful and there are useful online archives for the UK (**Search: Official Charts Company**) and the US (**Search: Billboard Chart Archive**) which will show a fair amount of detail of what was selling in any given year, month or week since the pop charts began.

If you want to go further back, or farther afield, then I recommend the oddly-named Radiooooo website, which has an interactive map enabling you to listen to music from 1900 onwards from a number of countries across the globe. Handy for research and also for atmosphere. (**Search: Radiooooo** with five Os)

The American Radio History website not only contains a vast archive of digitised magazines relating to radio and television broadcast and engineering but also covers similar publications from around the English-speaking world. Many of these are particularly fascinating for the advertising content, with music hardware, instruments and albums, new radio and TV shows advertised in their pages. (**Search: American Radio History**)

The BBC Genome Project contains all the *Radio Times* listings from 1923 to 2009, so is ideal if you want to work out what your character might have been watching on the telly one summer afternoon in 1976[19]. It also includes links to episodes and clips where available. (**Search: BBC Genome**)

Writing

The novelist Emma Darwin has a blog, 'This Itch of Writing', which is full of excellent and practical advice on writing. She has collected all the relevant posts in a section she calls the Tool Kit. I hesitate to send you in its direction as you'll probably think she explains it all much better than

---

19   In case you are curious, it could have been *Speed Buggy*, *Animal Magic*, *Lippy Lion*, or *Barbapapa*.

I do but you've bought and read this book now so it is too late. (**Search: Darwin Itch Tool Kit**)

Unsure how to capitalise your chapter titles? Which words need to start with a capital letter and which ones don't? There are many online tools to help you out but I tend to use capitalizemytitle.com despite its use of an -ize ending. (**Search: Capitalization Tool**)

Want to know how to pronounce a word? Try the Forvo website, which contains recordings of real people speaking words in their own languages. This can be handy when you want to get your head round words or phrases from languages other than your own, but also place names and the names of famous people. (**Search: Forvo**)

Research

Encylopaedia Britannica has been around for just over 250 years and has, thankfully, moved into the digital age, with a handy, searchable format. UK library-card holders can view pretty much the entirety of its content for free by logging in with their card number. (**Search: Encyclopaedia Brittanica**)

Likewise, a huge amount of Oxford University Press reference material is available for free to UK library-card holders, or on a subscription basis to others. It has a vast catalogue of reference books on more or less any subject you care to think of and individual entries can be viewed online. I just entered 'chocolate cake' to see what it came up with and was presented with articles and content about chocolate mud cake, Black Forest gateaux, lamingtons, eclairs, torte, numerous other baked goods and even a little-known Australian rock band called My Friend The Chocolate Cake. I probably shouldn't search while hungry. (**Search: Oxford Reference**)

Separate to the main Oxford Reference database is the Oxford Dictionary of National Biography, a massive ongoing project that contains biographical content on thousands of famous and notable Britons of the past. Do note, they have to be both British and dead to have an entry but that includes a hell of a lot of people, as well as, perhaps, a lot of people in hell. Some Irish figures are also included. This is another resource available free to library-card holders so, hey kids, join your local library pronto. (**Search: Oxford National Biography**)

The US Library of Congress has a useful searchable site that will link to free content as well as showing details of its own holdings. It has a wealth of digitised content that is free to view from anywhere in the world. It also groups material together by themes and categories so it can be enjoyable and informative to browse for material related to the topic you are writing about, or you can simply search for specific subjects. (**Search: Library of Congress**)

I also have to acknowledge the wonderful and completely free Wikipedia, which you will all be aware of already but there are very few subjects it doesn't cover. Do be warned, the content is not always accurate or verified – I am not allowed to use it as a source when writing my TV-show quiz questions, for example – but it is still a very handy general reference source. (**Search: Wikipedia**)

You may not be as aware of Wikimedia Commons, which is similar in look and layout to Wikipedia but contains a wealth of free media-content, such as images, sound recordings and videos. It can be particularly helpful for writers of non-fiction looking for picture content that won't cost anything to use. (**Search: Wiki Commons**)

Infoplease is another source of free encyclopaedia-type content and has a searchable database as well as content presented in themed categories. It also has an Ask the Editors FAQ section. (**Search: Infoplease**)

Although the CIA is best known for assassinating world leaders, organising coups and other hilarious shenanigans it has also compiled a very useful World Factbook which contains key facts on nearly every country in the world. This covers everything from official languages to topography, history, industry, population breakdown and density, agriculture and even sanitation. It is extremely useful for researching locations at a national level and can help you check whether a particular event or plot point would make sense in that particular place. The site also has lots of maps and other useful content. (**Search: CIA World Factbook**)

Wolfram Alpha is a different type of search engine. It is largely science- and maths-based and will only show content from curated and approved sites, gathering together factual information from each. For example, if I enter the search term 'diamond', I am presented with a short definition, followed by an image of a diamond, then a table of basic chemical and physical properties, a more detailed table of its crystallographic properties (no idea what anything in there meant) and finally a summary. A very useful way of presenting lots of factual data in an accessible fashion. (**Search: Wolfram Alpha**)

Google Ngram allows you to search for a particular term, phrase or name and then displays its frequency of use over time, referring to a pre-determined library of books, journals and articles. It also allows you to compare multiple sets of words or phrases. So you could enter 'buffoon', 'nincompoop' and 'bozo' and would find that buffoon was by far the most popular of the three words in the 1800s but that bozo has been catching it up in the last 50 years or so. This particular example is of no use to you whatsoever but it is a handy tool for comparisons of a less frivolous nature. (**Search: Google Ngram**)

If you are having trouble tracking down a book then worldcat.org is a database of libraries from around the world and will show you which libraries have it in stock. I just used it and found out that the nearest copy of my last book is 279km away in the National Library of Scotland. I knew there was a reason I'd always liked the Scots. (**Search: Worldcat**)

And someone, I know not who or why, has digitised loads of Argos catalogues from the 1970s onwards. Potentially very handy if you want to check products that were popular in certain years, or to remind yourself what they looked like or how much they cost. US readers won't have a clue what I am going on about. (**Search: Argos Book of Dreams**)

Likewise, someone is in the process of digitising loads of old copies of *Smash Hits*. (**Search: Smash Hits Archive**)

Freelancers

If you are looking for an editor, proofreader, typesetter, book-cover designer or someone to help with the marketing of your book then Reedsy is an excellent online marketplace for publishing freelancers. Essentially it is a site that allows authors to search and hire publishing professionals. You enter the sort of work you need doing and a list of pre-vetted and qualified people will appear, along with short bios and CVs. You can then select a few of them to send a request to, outlining the sort of work you need done. They reply with offers and you can choose who you want to work with. The whole thing, including payment and any contracts, is handled within Reedsy and it is a secure, safe environment. Reedsy only accept a tiny percentage of the freelancers who apply to be members, checking out their credentials and previous work. Most of the people on there offering services are people who have worked in the book world for some time. People like me. I strongly recommend Reedsy if you are looking for an editor to check your work before it goes to agents and publishers but there are a whole host of other excellent services you can make use of as well, including writing tutorials and even an online typesetting tool. (**Search: Reedsy**)

Support and services

The Society of Authors is sort of a writers' union, offering a variety of support services for authors, including legal advice on contracts and contract disputes as well as help on many aspects of life as a writer. They have plenty of members-only offers too. Open to writers across the world but they specialise in UK stuff when it comes to contracts and legal. (**Search: Society of Authors**)

Every time one of your books is borrowed from a UK library you are entitled to a payment of roughly 8p. This may sound like a tiny amount but, over time, it can add up, and the most-borrowed authors from libraries make a tidy sum from loans. However, you can only claim the money if you are registered with the Public Lending Rights system. It is simple to do; you just fill in some details about yourself and your books and they handle the rest. Many other countries have a version of PLR – so, worth investigating locally if you are not a UK resident. (**Search: PLR**)

Similarly, ALCS (Authors' Licensing and Collecting Society) is a not-for-profit organisation that collects author payments from around the world from things such as international library loans, educational photocopying and the like. There is a one-off fee but I made more than that back from my first payment. I was amazed by the amounts they were able to rustle up for me. (**Search: ALCS**)

19

Recommended Reading

Here are some publications you might find useful if you want to read more about the topics covered in this volume.

Emma Darwin – *Get Started in Writing Historical Fiction*

Emma is great at explaining the techniques and processes that go into writing good fiction and here she delves into her own specialist area of historical fiction. If this is a genre you are writing then I consider this book to be essential reading. It forms part of the *Teach Yourself* series of writing guides that cover most areas of fiction and non-fiction so do check out their full list of titles.

Stephen King – *On Writing*

Considered by many to be the ultimate insider's guide to the craft of writing from one of the bestselling authors of all time. Well worth reading even if you are not a fan of King's novels, or writing in the same genres as he does. There is lots in here that will help any writer.

Benjamin Dreyer – *Dreyer's English*

Dreyer is the head of copyediting for Random House in the US and this book contains heaps of practical advice on the nuts and bolts of writing, including examples of common mistakes and how to avoid them. It is also lots of fun and contains more than a few gossipy anecdotes about writers and publishing.

Will Storr – *The Science of Storytelling*

A relative newcomer to the field of books about writing but one that has garnered a lot of fans very quickly and seems to be destined to be part of every new writer's library. Storr examines the art of storytelling from ancient myths to modern box-set television, and prises out the lessons that writers can learn from all the various forms discussed.

Sam Leith – *Write to the Point*

An experienced journalist explains how best to get your message across through your writing. It isn't specifically about writing books but there is lots here that you could find useful, especially if you are writing non-fiction or any work where you are making an argument or presenting a case.

Joe Moran – *First You Write a Sentence*
An authoritative, but accessible, look at examples of great writing: the words and sentences that can spark wonder in readers. How have writers done this in the past and what can we all learn from them? This is another fairly recent book that has become a word-of-mouth success.

Sir Ernest Gowers & Rebecca Gowers – *Plain Words*
Ernest Gowers wrote a style guide for the UK civil service back in the 1950s and it was quickly adopted by the wider public because of its common-sense advice and great humour and charm. His great-granddaughter recently updated the content for the modern reader and writer. It remains a plain and simple guide full of practical advice.

Maryanne Wolf – *Proust and the Squid*
Subtitled *The Story and Science of the Reading Brain*, this book delves into the mechanics of reading from a scientific perspective and is a fascinating look at how and why humans read, despite the fact that we were not born to do so and have yet to evolve to do so. Although this may not have a direct influence on the plot of your novel, or the dialogue your characters speak, I do feel that a broader understanding of how the brain works when we read can help a writer in their overall approach to writing.

Stanislas Dehaene – *Reading in the Brain*
Another look at the science of reading, how we have grown to use black marks on a white page to interpret and understand the world around us. Like Wolf's book above, this is less

about writing and more about how and why people read – a subject many authors could benefit from learning more about.

Alan Jacobs – *The Pleasures of Reading in an Age of Distraction*

Finally, a book that explores the joy of reading in the 21st century. How books are competing against other visual and mental stimuli and how we, as readers, can manage the onslaught to our senses. I re-read this book every couple of years as it reminds me to step back, appreciate reading for the sake of it, to take off my editor's hat and just have fun with the stories authors tell.

20

Contact Details

I offer freelance editorial services including checking your submissions package, an editorial review of your manuscript and a full structural edit. I can also present much of the content of this book as a dynamic interactive workshop, complete with swearing, to your festival or writing group, whether in person or online. I can even act as a writing guide and mentor if you are looking for support on your publishing adventure. If you mention that you have bothered to read my book then I can offer you a 10% discount on all or any of my services.

You are also very welcome to drop me a line with any questions you have about the topics covered in this book.

Email: thatscottpack@gmail.com
Twitter: @meandmybigmouth
Reedsy: reedsy.com/scottpack

21

About the Author

Scott Pack was born in 1970 and grew up on an island in the River Thames (which was not quite as idyllic as it sounds). He spent the 1990s working at HMV, first in its record stores and latterly in its head office, leaving just before digital music took over.

He was head of buying for the Waterstones book chain for the first half of the 2000s, leaving just before ebooks became a big deal. He does not claim to have been a particularly notable retailer but he did have impeccable timing.

He was then a publisher at HarperCollins for several years – where he was the editor for authors including Brian Aldiss, Kristin Hersh, Andrew Kaufman, Niven Govinden and Eric Morecambe – before becoming a freelance editor and writer.

He acquires books for a number of independent publishers, including Eye & Lightning Books (who have produced this fine volume).

Scott has written three previous books under the pen-name of Steve Stack. *It Is Just You, Everything's Not Shit* is an A to Z of the nice things in life. *21st-Century Dodos* is a collection of amusing eulogies to inanimate objects on the verge of extinction; it spawned a festive off-shoot called *Christmas Dodos*. All three books are still available and likely to be found in secondhand shops up and down the land.

He has also written journalism for newspapers and magazines, including *Private Eye*, the *Guardian*, *The Times* and *Observer Magazine*. He has interviewed, live on stage, Haruki Murakami, Natalie Haynes, David Mitchell, WWE wrestler Mick Foley, Naomi Alderman and others. In print he has interviewed Simon Armitage, Oscar-winning actor Joel Grey, Kerry Hudson, Ray Robinson and Robert McCrum.

Scott is the co-founder, with Kat Stephen, of Abandoned Bookshop, a project that searches for forgotten and neglected books and re-issues them as print and ebooks. Together they have re-published books by Miles Gibson, Jules Verne, Rudyard Kipling, Norman Thomas di Giovanni, Grazia Deledda, Elizabeth Ironside and many more.

More recently, Scott has started writing questions for television quiz shows including *Fifteen to One*, *Impossible* and *Mastermind*. His specialist subject rounds for *Mastermind* range from Taylor Swift to Jean-Paul Sartre, from Manic Street Preachers to *The Mabinogion*, and from Douglas Adams to *Game of Thrones*.

He works from his home in Windsor and is rarely far

from some tea and cake. He wouldn't normally include a biography of this length in one of his books but there were some spare pages at the end that needed filling.

22

Acknowledgements

My thanks to:

Everyone at Eye & Lightning books for their support, patience and helpful interjections, and for allowing me to deliver the manuscript way later than would normally be acceptable.

The splendid people whose names adorn the cover and opening pages of this book alongside the generous quotes they provided. I have found it is much easier to get a quote for your book if the person you are asking doesn't have to read it.

Scores of people on Twitter who offered feedback on everything from the book's subtitle to the FAQs and resources, and who were just generally supportive of the project over the past year or so. And a special mention for Barbara, a much-loved and much-missed Twitter friend who got behind so many of my endeavours and tolerated my swearing.

I usually thank my family but I wrote all of this while they weren't around *and* I cooked all the dinners so, basically, they should be thanking me.

Kat for reading and offering suggestions. Chances are you are watching an episode of *The Office* right now. Or perhaps *Tiny House Nation*. I hope you are enjoying it.

Rebecca for also reading and also offering suggestions. May your otters always be at rest.

Ida Wenøe, San Fermin, Gia Margaret, Aldous Harding, Yasmine Hamdan, Nina Kinert, This is the Kit, Aisha Badru, Fenne Lily and Slow Meadow for providing the soundtrack to the writing of this book.

The Danish, for their pastries, and Tunnock's, for their caramel wafers.